developing literacy

Young Children's
Use of Language

Edited by
Robert P. Parker
Rutgers University
and
Frances A. Davis
Beaver College

Published by the
INTERNATIONAL READING ASSOCIATION
800 Barksdale Road, Box 8139, Newark, Delaware 19714

INTERNATIONAL READING ASSOCIATION

Copyright 1983 by the
International Reading Association, Inc.

Library of Congress Cataloging in Publication Data
Main entry under title:

Developing literacy.

Includes bibliographies.
1. Children—Language—Addresses, essays, lectures.
2. Language arts—Addresses, essays, lectures.
I. Parker, Robert P. (Robert Prescott), 1937-
II. Davis, Frances R. A.
LB1139.L3D494   1983   372.6   82-20329
ISBN 0-87207-531-1

Second Printing, August 1985

ii

Contents

Foreword   *v*

1 PART ONE   BASES FOR LITERACY: SOCIAL AND COGNITIVE
3 Adult Assistance to Language Development: Scaffolds, Models, and
Direct Instruction   *Courtney B. Cazden*
19 Thinking and Experience: The Cognitive Base for Language Experience
Irene Athey

35 PART TWO   BEGINNINGS OF LITERACY: TALKING, WRITING, READING
38 Language Development and Learning to Write: Theory and Research Findings
Robert P. Parker
55 Children's Use of Language and Learning to Read   *Joan Tough*
68 Beginning Reading Development: Strategies and Principles
Yetta M. Goodman

85 PART THREE   WRITING AND READING: WHAT FOR?
87 Creating Minds, Created Texts: Writing and Reading
June Birnbaum and *Janet Emig*
105 Writing: What For?   *Nancy Martin*
118 The Reading Transaction: What For?   *Louise M. Rosenblatt*

137 PART FOUR   SCHOOLING AND LITERACY
139 Schooling and the Growth of Mind   *Robert P. Parker*
156 Developing Literacy: Observation, Analysis, and Mediation in Schools
Frances A. Davis
173 Reading and Writing in the Real World: Explorations into the Culture of Literacy
David M. Smith

iv

Foreword

"Reading as a thinking process" has long been a phrase popular with certain authorities in the field of reading. If questioned, these authorities probably would agree that the phrase, "language as a thinking process," would be just as reasonable. The authors of this volume, however, have based this discussion on the latter phrase—*language* as a thinking process.

The papers here investigate the relationships among all aspects of language—reading, writing, speaking, and listening. Furthermore, the authors of the chapters in this volume recognize that language itself is not an isolated entity, but part of a larger social cultural and cognitive context. This expanded context then forms the definition of what we call literacy.

Literacy, though, is not dealt with in the abstract; rather, the focus is the development of language in young children. Issues related to this theme are explored from the many different viewpoints of the researchers, the teacher, the psychologist, and the anthropologist. Studies from several countries are analyzed and synthesized to form the theoretical constructs presented here. From these constructs are generated some guiding principles or models under which "older people" should function in helping young children become literate.

In a time when we still have publishers, researchers, and teachers continually isolating the components of the language process, this volume should be required reading for all persons involved in helping young children develop language facility.

Jack Cassidy, President
International Reading Association
1982-1983

Part One
Bases for Literacy:
Social and Cognitive

How do children develop competence in the discourse forms valued in schools, particularly those which comprise "essayist" literacy? And how do older children and adults assist with this development? Courtney Cazden addresses these questions in her paper, describing three ways in which older people typically and naturally provide such assistance. She calls them scaffolds, models, and direct instruction. Each of these forms of assistance, as it appears in the home, contributes directly to children's discourse development, and each has its close counterpart in the classroom. For example, the basic structure of adult-child book reading interaction, categorized here as one sort of scaffold, closely resembles the "turn-allocation procedures" used by teachers.

Though these forms of assistance are more distinct in theory than in practice, an understanding of their differences (as Cazden presents them) provides a useful perspective for teachers both on some important social dimensions of children's preschool language development and on the ways interactions in classrooms may be structured to provide further assistance. As long as certain forms of discourse constitute valued learning in schools, it is important for us to be clear about what these forms are, how children naturally are assisted in their mastery, and how we as educators might fit our efforts into this picture.

Irene Athey takes a different tack in her paper. Rather than emphasizing the contribution of certain forms of social interaction to language development, Athey discusses the ways in which cognitive structures (forms of cognition?) provide a basis for children's development in the use of language as a symbol system. Her particular concern is with the relationship between cognitive structure and the child's use of language to construct meaning from experience.

To understand this relationship better, Athey contends, we need to extend our research beyond the experimental and quantitative into the realm of the naturalistic and qualitative. Only then will we be able, for example, to understand fully the nature of reading as a thinking process, and of concept development as an important aspect of that process. Athey notes that scheme theory is a recent manifestation of this alternative theoretical view, just as language experience was an earlier one. As such, it provides new opportunities for looking into the relationship between cognition and symbol use.

Together, these papers present a broad perspective on the social and cognitive aspects of language development, and on their implications for research and teaching.

Adult Assistance to Language Development: Scaffolds, Models, and Direct Instruction[1]

Courtney B. Cazden
Harvard University

In her beautiful book on the problems of inexperienced adult writers, Mina Shaughnessy writes of their difficulty in composing passages "beyond the sentence:"

> "There is not a sentence," writes Whitehead, "which adequately states its own meaning." The statement suggests that the quality of an idea is not to be found in a nucleus or thesis statement but in the sentences that follow or lead up to that statement. An idea, in this sense, is not a "point" so much as a branching tree of elaboration and demonstration.
> This distinction is useful in approaching the difficulties BW [Basic Writer] students have beyond the sentence, for it is accurate to say, although many teachers say it, that BW students have no ideas, if by "idea" they mean what is conventionally meant by an "idea"—that is, a "point" or general statement. Not only do BW students produce essays that are full of points but the points they make are often the same ones that more advanced writers make when writing on the same subject. The differences lie in the style and extent of elaboration (1977, p. 226).

Shaughnessy is talking about the particular forms of elaboration expected in academic discourse: the convention of ranging widely but predictably between cases and generalizations, and the conventions of marking the rhetorical relationships between larger units of composition (1980). But these problems must have their antecedents in earlier school years, and be open to help then too.

Consider two sharing time narratives from a California first grade observed by Michaels and Cook-Gumperz (1979).

They identify two styles by which sentences are combined into a larger oral text: topic-centered and topic-chaining.

Topic-centered		*Topic-chaining*	
Jenny:	Yesterday	Deena:	I went to the beach Sunday
	my mom		and to McDonald's
	and my whole family		and to the park
	went with me to a party		and I got this for my birthday
	and it was a Thanksgiving		My mother bought it for me
	party		and I had two dollars for
	where and we		my birthday
*St. T:	mm		and I put it in here
Jenny:	my mom		and I went to where my friend
	we had to get dress up as		named Gigi
	Pilgrims		I went over to my grand-
	and my mom made me this		mother's house with her
	hat for a Pilgrim		and she was on my back
St. T:	Oh great.		and I and we was walking
			around
			by my house
			and she was heavy
			She was in the sixth or
			seventh grade
		St. T:	Ok I'm going to stop you.
			I want you to talk about
			things that are really, really
			very important (1979,
			pp. 8-10).

Whereas Jenny's topic-centered narrative receives a confirming "Oh great," Deena's topic-chain is cut off with criticism for what the teacher refers to as her "filibuster." Despite the teacher's insensitivity, and her egocentric notion of what's really important, Jenny's narrative (with its greater detail about a single event) is more interesting to listen to or to read. Even though Deena is one of the best readers in the class, her "topic-chaining oral discourse style may, in time, greatly interfere with her ability to produce literate sounding descriptive prose" (1979, p. 12).

As with many language abilities, the ability to construct such prose develops very early in supportive environments. As

*Student Teacher

one example of what is possible, here is the Scollons' account of their daughter Rachel's ability to tell the kind of narratives they, like Michaels and Cook-Gumperz, believe to be related to later acquisition of literacy in school. A few days before her third birthday, Rachel silently "wrote" a story in circular scribbles and then "read" it to her parents. Here's the story, with division into lines to indicate pauses, dots (.) to indicate breaths, and double slashes (//) to indicate an intonation contour of high rise and then fall, which serves to close an information unit and yet communicate an intention to continue reading.

There was a b-
girl
she
went out to get snow//
.
she
she made a hole//
.
she
.
she went back
she cried//
she went back in tell m-
.
her
her mom to get
tel--old her Mom, to
hive her apple//
so she gived her apple//
.
she got
.
she went out again
got sn-
some more snow//

(Scollon & Scollon, 1979, pp. 12-13)

Rachel's ability to tell a third person narrative about an incident in her own life a few days before is impressive. Note her self-corrections from "M-" to "her Mom" and from "tell" to "told." Understandably, problems remain: the referents for the same sex pronouns in "she gived her apple" are ambiguous, but that specific problem in anaphora persists well into the elementary years anyway (Bartlett, 1980).

While most discussions of oral preparations for what the Scollons call "essayist" literacy focus on what children learn from being read to and being around adults and older children who read and write frequently and happily, they acknowledge such influences and go beyond to suggest what additional assistance Rachel received through adult-child interaction. I'll report their observations and then generalize to three broad kinds of adult assistance that I call scaffolds, models, and direct instruction— first with examples from young children's language development at home, and then at school.

Scaffolds

A scaffold is a temporary framework for construction in progress. Psycholinguistically, the term "scaffold" was first used by Jerome Bruner to characterize adult assistance to children's language development.

One kind of scaffold is what the Scollons call "vertical constructions," in which the adult asks the child for additional new information in each utterance. The result has what Bruner calls a ratchet-like quality (personal communication, 1980) with the adult helping to "hold" each previous utterance in focal attention while asking the child to say more.[2] In the Scollons' words:

> The child says something. The mother asks about it and the child says something further. The first can be seen as a topic statement, the mother's comment as a request for a comment, and the child's answer as giving that comment.
>
> As the child develops she begins to take over both roles. That is, Brenda [the subject of R. Scollon's previous study, 1976] soon began to say both the topic and the comment. As soon as these became prosodically linked as a single utterance the whole process shifted up a level. The whole topic-comment pair was taken as a given and the interlocutor sought another comment. An example of one of these more elaborate pairs follows:

> | Brenda: | Tape recorder |
> |---------|---------------|
> | | Ue it |
> | | Use it |
> | Int.: | Use it for what? |
> | Brenda: | Talk |
> | | corder talk |
> | | Brenda talk |

Two things are important for this discussion. One is that this development is based on interaction with other speakers. The other is that it involves the progressive incorporation within a single tone group of greater amounts of new information (Scollon & Scollon, 1979, pp. 43-44).

R. Scollon first described "vertical constructions" in his study of Brenda (1976). At that time he believed them to provide assistance to the child's development of syntax. Because of intervening evidence from other researchers that children develop syntax in the absence of this particular form of interaction, the Scollons now believe that "The vertical construction is a discourse process as is the information structuring of essayist literacy. We now see the former as an important means of teaching the latter" (1979, p. 45).

The interaction with Brenda is about the tape recorder, present at the moment of speaking. New problems confront the child who, like Rachel, is struggling to encode a narrative of a past event. Stoel-Gammon and Cabral (1977) describe the development of the "reportative function" in Brazilian children 20-24 months old. Attempts to construct narratives of past experiences usually occur first in a dialogue in which the adult asked questions that acted as prompts. For example, when a 20-month-old child reported "Fell ground," the adult prompted more information by asking how and where it happened and "Who pushed you down?" These early reports were most successful when the adult had been with the child at the event and later asked the child to relate what had happened to a third person. The questions of a companion not only elicit progressively more information from the child, they also indicate to the child what aspects of the past event are significant and notable, focusing the child's mental image on those aspects that should be replayed in the present account.

Another kind of interactional scaffold appears in adult-child conversations in these early years (in proto-conversations with infants, and in the language games such as peekaboo and picture-book reading) where the adult creates a sequential structure with slots of certain shapes in which the child comes to speak. In a different domain, that of learning to play a musical instrument, comparable assistance is supplied by special chamber music records, called "add-a-part" or "music minus one," each with a missing part to be played to the novice, in a graduated series of difficulty. Neither scaffolds nor add-a-part records are as dynamic and interactional as these language games; moreover, the games are very special scaffolds in self-destructing gradually as the need lessens, to be replaced by a new support for a more elaborate construction. But if these limitations are kept in mind, both metaphors may be helpful.

In proto-conversations with infants, mothers work hard to maintain a conversation with their 3 to 18-month-old babies, despite the inadequacies of their conversational partners (Snow, 1977). At first they accept burps, yawns, and coughs as well as laughs and coos—but not arm-waving or head movements—as the baby's turn. They fill in for the babies by asking and answering their own questions, and by phrasing questions so that a minimal response can be treated as a reply. By seven months, when the babies become more active, the mothers no longer accept all the baby's vocalizations, only vocalic or consonantal babbles. As the mother raises the ante, the child's development proceeds.

In peekaboo and picture-book reading, as in the proto-conversations, the adult first produces the entire script, then gradually relinquishes parts as the child develops the ability to speak them. In peekaboo, the mother starts by doing the hiding (usually herself) as well as the talking—answering as well as asking questions about who and where. The child gradually takes over the actions and then the speech, reverses roles and asks, "Where's Mommy?" Finally, there is a solo performance with objects the child has made to disappear (Ratner & Bruner, 1978).

As peekaboo is a routinized speech situation, structured around the physical activities of hiding and finding, so picture-book is a ritualized speech event, where talk is the primary purpose—not just phatic communication and greetings as in peekaboo, but labeling for which the book provides clear and present referents. In one common form, book reading in the children's second year has a four-part structure:

An attentive vocative, such as *Look*.
A query, such as *What's that?*
A label, such as *It's an X*.
A feedback utterance, such as *Yes, that's an X*
(if the child has provided the label) [paraphrased from Ninio & Bruner, 1978, p. 6].

As the child's development proceeds, the adult encourages the child to speak more of the script.

A larger set of early language games played by 9 English and 16 Dutch families has been analyzed by Snow, Dubber, and de Blauw, and their analysis confirms and extends that of Bruner and his colleagues. Their conclusions speak to the benefits of the scaffolds provided in all these routinized situations.

> Several years ago, in a study of social class differences in mothers' speech (Snow, Arlman-Rupp, Hassing, Jobse, Joosten, & Vorster, 1976), we found that mothers' speech was more complex in a book-reading than a free-play situation. We suggested then that this resulted from the greater contextual support for speech available during book reading; the presence of the book served to focus attention and determine topics, so these tasks need not be fulfilled by maternal utterances. The automatic establishment of joint attention to an agreed upon topic freed the mother to make more sophisticated, and thus linguistically more complex, comments than would be possible during free play.
>
> While this explanation cannot be ruled out, I now feel that a much more potent reason for the greater complexity of "book talk" can be found in the accompanying routinization. Routines enable participants to deal with complexity. We think of routines as simple and unsophisticated—the product of memory, not of rule use. But their simplicity allows for the introduction, into the slots created by the routine, of fillers considerably more complex in structure and/or content than could possibly be dealt with elsewhere. The slot, by its predictability, provides the opportunity for novel, complex, and creative fillers to be inserted (1980, pp. 13-14).

Thus, the two kinds of scaffolds—vertical constructions and game-like routines—provide different kinds of support for the child's growing ability in both language and social interactions.

Before turning to the second kind of assistance, the provision of models, it is important to think about the similarities and differences between these scaffolds at home and at school.

In formal terms, similarities between the basic book reading structure and classroom lessons (Mehan, 1979) are striking. With the mother's attentional vocative replacing the teacher's turn-allocation procedures, the remaining parts of the book-reading event fit exactly the initiation-reply-evaluation sequence of the lessons. Moreover, the initiations in both events are questions to which the adult asker knows the answer. In studies of antecedents of school success, many people have found a high correlation between being read to and succeeding in school, and have remarked on the special linguistic features of written text (C. Chomsky, 1972) or of the conversation interpolated into the text-reading scene (Snow, 1980). The structural similarities suggest that picture-book reading may, in addition to its substantive contribution, be the basis for transfer to participation in the discourse structure of classroom lessons several years later.

But there are differences too: Classroom lessons are notably less responsive to the child's growing competence. Instead of self-destructing, the structure remains much the same across grades, and only the content of the slots—the teacher's questions and students' answers—increase in complexity. Furthermore, students do not get a chance to take over the adult role. For such opportunities, peer dialogues are essential.[3]

There can be an analogue to "interference," or negative transfer, between earlier and later discourse patterns in this early learning. As Ninio and Bruner point out, picture-book reading has a different structure if the mother reads a nursery rhyme and leaves a slot for the child to fill in at the end of each line. A graduate student at Harvard, Sharon Haselkorn, reported interference between the patterns of mother and researcher that she encountered over book reading at this early age. Sharon is used to playing the What's That? game, but one of her young subjects had learned the Fill-in-the-Blank game, and they had a very hard time getting their speech event together (personal communication, 1978). Even very young children are acculturated beings, and these cultural differences increase in importance by school age. Part of the reason that Deena's teacher evaluates her narrative ability so negatively, and does not help Deena with interpolated questions as she does Jenny, may be because of a mismatch in expectations (Michael & Cook-Gumperz, 1979).

Models

As we talk to children, how we speak indicates how texts are constructed for particular purposes and in particular situations. In adopting the term *model* for a child's form of assistance, we must remember that the child's task is to acquire an underlying structure; imitation of the model itself does not suffice. The texts we supply are examples to learn from, not samples to copy.[4]

Caretakers who are literate themselves not only supply models through reading to children, but also coach young children in such narrative accounting by speaking for them before they can speak for themselves—by giving a running account of an activity as it is taking place: "See, look, we throw it up and we catch it. . . ."; or by telling the child a story about herself after an event has taken place, "Once upon a time there was a little girl named Rachel. . . ." (Scollon & Scollon, 1979).

Such narratives, the Scollons believe, help the child develop what they call "fictionalization of the self": the ability to distance oneself from participation in an event and as an observer describe it to someone else. By extension, the provision of such models—jokes and arguments as well as narratives—should aid the acquisition of the structure of different genres of oral and written texts. Knowledge of such structures is not only necessary for composition, but can make that composition an easier task by providing some decisions ready made (Bartlett, 1980).

Of course, models and scaffolds are much less separate in conversation than they are in theory; and in practice they should be deliberately combined to help children learn the particular discourse forms valued in school. One excellent example of such a combination comes from Heath's work (1982) with teachers in a southeastern United States black community she calls Trackton. When the teachers complained that the Trackton children did not participate in lessons, Heath helped them understand what she had learned from five years of ethnographic field work in the Trackton community. For example, the children were not used to known-answer questions about the labels and attributes of objects and events. As one third grade boy complained, "Ain't nobody can talk about things being about theirselves." Heath then worked with the teachers to try out changes in their classrooms, in the following sequence:

Start with familiar content, and with familiar kinds of talk about that content.

Go on to new kinds of talk, still about the familiar content, and provide peer models, available for rehearing on audio cassettes.

Provide opportunities for the Trackton children to practice the new kinds of talk, first out of the public arena and also on tape, and then in actual lessons.

Finally, talk with the children about talk itself.

Because Heath's work offers such an imaginative and rare example of assitance to children's discourse development in school, I quote at some length her description of these four steps:

For some portions of the curriculum, teachers adapted some teaching materials and techniques in accordance with what they had learned about questions in Trackton. For example, in early units on social studies, which taught about "our community," teachers began to use photographs of sections of different local communities, public buildings of the town, and scenes from the nearby countryside. Teachers then asked not for the identification of specific objects or attributes of the objects in these photographs, but questions such as:

What's happening here?

Have you ever been here?

Tell me what you did when you were there.

What's this like? (pointing to a scene, or item in a scene)

Responses of children were far different than those given in usual social studies lessons. Trackton children talked, actively and aggressively became involved in the lesson, and offered useful information about their past experiences. For specific lessons, responses of children were taped; after class, teachers then added to the tapes specific questions and statements identifying objects, attributes, etc. Answers to these questions were provided by children adept at responding to these types of questions. Class members then used these tapes in learning centers. Trackton students were particularly drawn to these, presumably because they could hear themselves in responses similar in type to those used in their own community. In addition, they benefitted from hearing the kinds of questions and answers teachers used when talking about things. On the tapes, they heard appropriate classroom discourse strategies. Learning these strategies from tapes was less threatening than acquiring them in actual classroom activities where the facility of other students with recall questions enabled them to dominate teacher-student interactions. Gradually, teachers asked specific Trackton students to work with them in preparing recall questions and answers to add to the tapes. Trackton students then began to hear *themselves* in successful classroom responses to questions such as "What is that?" "What kind of community helper works there?"

In addition to using the tapes, teachers openly discussed different types of questions with students, and the class talked about the kinds of answers called for by certain questions. For example, *who, when,* and *what* questions could often be answered orally by single words; other kinds of questions were often answered with many words which made up sentences and paragraphs when put to writing (Heath, 1982).

Ideally, we should provide opportunities for children to practice a growing range of discourse functions (explaining, narrating, instructing) first in situations where models and supports are available, then gradually with less help. Imagine the kind of help Heath's teachers gave children for answering questions and being available for the children telling narratives in the classroom observed by Michaels and Cook-Gumperz. One might start with narratives about content known to the teacher—as in retelling stories or reporting on a classroom trip—and then go to narratives of children's personal experiences where the teacher's guiding questions necessarily must be more general. For such assistance, the typical "show-and-tell" or "sharing time" is probably not the most helpful event. For children like Jenny, who don't need help, it is fine. But for children like Deena, the teacher needs more private time to give sustained help without worrying about losing the attention of the rest of the class; and Deena, like the Trackton children, needs a more private time in which to try.

Direct Instruction

The third kind of adult assistance is direct instruction, in which the adult not only models a particular utterance but directs the child to *say* or *tell* or *ask*. In spontaneous adult-child conversations, direct instruction seems to focus on two aspects of language development: appropriate social language use and correct vocabulary.

As Peekaboo is the prototypical scaffold, so "Say bye-bye" is the prototype of direct instruction. As described by Gleason and Weintraub, "Even when the child is only expected to open and close its fist, the adult, who may shake the baby's arm, is liable to say, "Say 'Bye-bye' " (1976, p. 130). Other routines considered important for polite social life and taught in this way are greetings, thanks, and other farewells, as well as routines for special occasions such as "trick or treat" on Halloween (Greif & Gleason, 1980).

But direct instruction is not limited to teaching children to be polite; it seems to be used to teach whatever interpersonal uses of language are considered essential for young children in a particular community. In some families, the focus will be on learning to be polite; in others, the focus may be on learning to speak in self-defense.

For example, Miller (1979) heard poignant examples of how three young white working-class mothers in South Baltimore taught their young children appropriate compliance and assertiveness in what they know to be a harsh world. One form of this instruction is giving the children lines to say to a third person, sometimes in play situations with dolls. For example, when 5 year old Kris took a doll from Amy, Marlene (the mother) helped Amy to reassert her claim by giving her the appropriate lines to say:

Amy	Marlene
	Oh, what did she [Kris] do?
my baby	
	Tell her [Kris], say "Keep off."
keep off	
keep off	
	Say "You hurt it."
you hurt it	
	(Miller, 1979, p. 115).

Preschool teachers often consider it part of their role to teach appropriate interpersonal language, such as how to substitute speech (assertive, but politely so) for physical action or cries. In a toddler class in one day care center, Isler observed that if a child begins to cry when another child attempts to pull a toy away, the teacher might intervene, "Can you use words and tell him/her 'I'm using this'?" (1980). In three observations in this class in November, December, and March, Isler followed the teachers' instructions and their results. In general, the children's cries and one word holophrases decreased and phrases increased. More interesting were the qualitative differences between November and the two later observations:

> The phrases recorded in November tended to be those which were frequently modeled in the class, such as "I using that," "Don't do it," and "Is mine" (or variations of those forms). Although the children certainly used all of these forms in December and March their repertoire seemed to have expanded considerably. Phrases recorded in December included "I sitting right here," "Too heavy people" (child was telling another child not to sit in a wagon she was pulling), "No banging floor," and "I eating that cracker." Phrases recorded in March included, "Becca's sleeping on me," "I wanna go there now," and "Dat not for you, dat is for Jonathan." It appears as if the children may not only learn the phrases modeled by the teachers but may also learn to recognize the situations in which it is appropriate to use verbal assertations. This understanding of the situational characteristics of language might then allow the child to expand his communicative skills as his vocabulary grows (Isler, 1980).

As with all models, children must generalize beyond the particular utterances and the particular situations in which the instruction is provided; and in these reports of direct instruction in real-life situations there is clear evidence that such generalizations take place. Whether direct instruction is effective in school recitations of more cognitive uses of language—as in the Distar program (Osborn & Becker, 1980)—is a more difficult question.[5]

The second focus of direct instruction in spontaneous adult-child conversations is vocabulary. In conversations about first-hand experience and in book reading, adults often say, "That's an X. Can you say X?" This is undoubtedly useful assistance, as long as we remember that direct instruction can give only the word itself, a seed from which rich conceptual meanings must grow more slowly. In Brown's felicitous phrase, the word is "an invitation to a concept" (Brown, 1958), inviting attention to itself and to the related verbal and nonverbal context when it is heard again; but it must be heard again and again, and in varying contexts as well.

In conclusion

While most of my examples of adult assistance are from middle-class families in the United States, I want to suggest that the kinds of assistance I have called scaffolds, models, and direct instruction are universally provided, with the particulars of each varying from culture to culture. For whatever behavior is considered important, adults will provide scaffold-like frameworks within which children at an early age can participate in weaving or fishing or speaking. Either as part of these scaffolds or separately, models of more mature behavior are always available as long as children have the opportunity to be around more competent members of the community, even if only as onlookers and eavesdroppers. Where direct instruction to "do" or "say" is given, that is probably an especially significant indicator of valued learning.

Footnotes

[1]Previous versions of this paper were presented during 1980 at conferences sponsored by the Federation Advisory Council on Early Childhood Education in Dallas; the Communications Arts Unit of the New York City Board of Education Office of Curriculum Development and Support; Brooklyn College Day Care Project; Rutgers University Graduate School of Education and IRA; and the Kentucky Association of Children under Six. I am grateful to participants in all these conferences for their questions and comments.

[2]In *Metaphors We Live By*, Lakoff and Johnson discuss how "we tend to structure the less concrete and inherently vaguer concepts (like those for the emotions) in terms of more concrete concepts, which are more clearly delineated in our experience" (1980, p. 112). In keeping with the directionality they point out, I am using the concepts of scaffold and rachet from the more concrete domains of construction and tool use to conceptualize the vaguer domain of interaction.

[3]A complementary paper to this one (Cazden, 1980) discusses the value of three kinds of peer dialogues: peer tutoring, equal status collaboration, and a hybrid form in which children take turns being resources for one another.

⁴Two more comments on models. First, for those of us who want to argue for the value of models of language provided in the texts of book we read aloud, see French philosopher J.P. Sartre's beautiful description of his first encounter with reading aloud in his autobiography, *The Words* (1964, pp. 28-30). In a one-room schoolhouse, even the readers of the older children can provide models for the younger children who listen. So claims author Rebecca Caudill in an autobiographical TV show, "Child of Appalachia."

Second, sometimes it seems that passages are learned by heart, and later analyzed into component structures. A friend wrote of the assistance she received through apartment walls in learning to play the piano some fifty years ago:

"I lived in the Bronx in the apartment above his (a young music student) on 169th Street—when he was about 14 or 15, studying at the Institute of Musical Art. He was a promising young musician even then....I also was one of those piano-study children, very musical but without whatever it was he had in addition—sittability, for one thing....I used to learn his repertoire [and] I was able years later to sail through those particular works I had heard him practice, as I had learned them by ear and had later acquired the necessary technique to play them as well. In particular I learned the Schumann Etudes Symphoniques, the Mendelssohn Concerto in G minor, and the Chopin Scherzo in B-flat minor. After that he moved and I had to do my own learning!" (personal communication, 1980).

⁵A related issue (not discussed in this paper), is how any of these forms of adult assistance function in second language teaching in school.

References

Bartlett, E.J. *Learning to write: Some cognitive and linguistic components.* Washington, D.C.: Center for Applied Linguistics, 1980.

Brown, R. *Words and things.* Glencoe, Illinois: Free Press, 1958.

Cazden, C.B. Peer dialogues across the curriculum. Paper presented at fourth conference on the impact of child language development research on curriculum and instruction, annual convention of the National Council of Teachers of English, Cincinnati, November 1980.

Cazden, C.B., Carrasco, R., Maldonado-Guzman, A.A., & Erickson, F. The contribution of ethnographic research to bicultural bilingual education. In J. Alatis (Ed.), *Current issues in bilingual education.* Washington, D.C.: Georgetown University Press, 1980.

Cazden, C.B., John, V.P., & Hymes, D. (Eds.). *Functions of language in the classroom.* New York: Teachers College Press, 1972.

Chomsky, C. Stages in language development and reading exposure. *Harvard Educational Review,* 1972, *42.*

Gleason, J.B., & Weintraub, S. The acquisition of routines in child language: Trick or treat. *Language in Society,* 1976, *5.*

Greif, E.B., & Gleason, J.B. Hi, thanks, and goodbye: More routine information. *Language in Society,* 1980, *9.*

Heath, S.B. Questioning at home and at school. In G. Spindler (Ed.), *Doing the ethnography of schooling: Educational anthropology in action.* New York: Holt, Rinehart and Winston, 1982.

Isler, L. Teacher's modeling of specific verbal behaviors and toddler's social interactions. Unpublished term paper, Harvard Graduate School of Education, 1981.

Lakoff, G., & Johnson, M. *Metaphors we live by.* Chicago: University of Chicago Press, 1980.

Mehan, H. *Learning lessons.* Cambridge, Massachusetts: Harvard University Press, 1979.
Michaels, S., & Cook-Gumperz, J. A study of sharing time with first grade students: Discourse narratives in the classroom. Berkeley Linguistics Society, 1979.
Miller, P.J. *Amy, Wendy and Beth: Language learning in south Baltimore.* Austin: University of Texas Press, 1982.
Ninio, A., & Bruner, J. The achievement and antecedents of labeling. *Journal of Child Language*, 1978, *5.*
Osborn, J., & Becker, W.C. Direct instruction language. *New Directions for Exeptional Children*, 1980, *2.*
Ratner, N., & Bruner, J. Games, social exchange and the acquisition of language. *Journal of Child Language*, 1978, *5.*
Sartre, J.P. *The words.* New York: Fawcett, 1964.
Scollon, R. *Conversations with a one year old: A case study of the developmental foundation of syntax.* Honolulu: University Press of Hawaii, 1976.
Shaughnessy, M.P. *Errors and expectations: A guide for the teacher of basic writing.* New York: Oxford University Press, 1977.
Snow, C.E. The development of conversation between mothers and babies. *Journal of Child Language*, 1977, *4.*
Snow, C.E., Dubber, C., & de Blauw, A. Routines in mother-child interaction. Unpublished manuscript, 1980.
Snow, C.E., Arlmann-Rupp, A., Hassing, Y., Jobse, J., Joosten, J., & Vorster, J. Mother's speech in three social classes. *Journal of Psycholinguistic Research*, 1976, *5.*
Stoel-Gammon, C., & Cabral, L.S. Learning how to tell it like it is: The development of the reporative function in children's speech. *Papers and Reports of Child Language Development*, 1977, *13.*

Thinking and Experience:
The Cognitive Base for Language Experience

Irene Athey
Rutgers University

Alexander Solzhenitsyn has noted: "One thing is absolutely definite; not everything that enters our ears penetrates our consciousness." As a psychologist, I ask myself why we do not readily or accurately translate the words that bombard us into the ideas they signify. As an educator, I ask myself what implications this slippage has for the transmission of information (I use information in its broadest sense here to include the learning of facts, concepts, rules, and social knowledge). In this paper, I will address the question of what this may mean for the language experience approach to reading.

To speak of the cognitive base for language experience suggests that cognition and language are two modes of behavior—two modes of learning about the world and operating in it in some way—which can, at least conceptually, be interfaced, seen in some relationship (temporal or causal) and, therefore, separated in theory if not in practice. I want to examine this assumption to see where it leads, and to think about why it may or may not be profitable for teachers to make this distinction. To what extent does this conceptual mechanism aid our understanding? These domains are figments of the psychologist's imagination and the issue here is whether this one is useful.

Let us begin by examining the newborn infant. This squirming blob does not come neatly compartmentalized into physical, cognitive, linguistic, and social components. It comes to us as a whole system, including an already well-developed brain which is a finely tuned instrument for receiving, discriminating, interpreting, and reconstructing signals from the environment into shapes and forms. Movements and sounds appear to have particular salience for the infant, in the sense that they are aspects of the surrounding scene that intrude on the senses. Human faces and voices readily attract the infant, as might be expected since movement and sound are vivid and immediate features of the human presence. However, the infant appears to perceive familiar voices as attributes of the configurations with which they are regularly associated. A strange voice attached to a familiar face is disturbing and will evoke crying, whereas the mother's voice is welcome even coming from the face of a stranger. Here we have, not the beginnings of object permanence, but the association of certain qualities regularly appearing together, an association that would seem to be a necessary prerequisite of object permanence.

Forming associations between sensory events is probably the most primitive and the earliest form of learning. Gagne (1970) characterized this as signal learning. It results from the regularity with which certain events occur together. Philosophers as early as Aristotle remarked on the principle of association, and the British empiricists (notably Locke) elevated the principle to the status of a theory with its own set of laws (vividness, recency, frequency). Under the term "association of ideas" Locke subsumed what we would today call cognitive events— sensations, perceptions, images, memories, and concepts, as well as ideas. Although Gagne couches signal learning in terms of stimuli and responses, he has clearly clothed the doctrine of association in modern terms. Associative learning permits the development of a set of predictions that becomes a stable part of the child's mental repertoire. Not all of these predictions are immutable. Piaget's work suggests that young children favor associations based on spatial proximity, and will attribute causality or belongingness to two objects or events solely on that basis. Eventually, through additional experience, the child discriminates essential from incidental qualities, and thus takes one more step toward acquiring object permanence and the more advanced concepts that depend on it.

Signal learning thus constitutes a major portion of the cognitive equipment acquired by the young child before the age of 3. It functions in enabling the child to predict forthcoming events and, hence, to impose some measure of order on an otherwise chaotic universe. Thus, the child's view of the universe, which emerges from the interaction of the brain with the events that impinge on it, is a construction that will undergo continuous growth and change as a result of new experiences and new constructions. But for the time being, the infant's functional behavior consists of associations built up through repeated simultaneous occurrences. At this stage, language is but one aspect of the child's encounters with the physical and social world. The child may respond to language as a thing in itself (an unconditioned stimulus as Pavlov would say) or to language as a signal of something else (a conditioned stimulus). The nonverbal aspects of language may be the most salient during this period. Psychologists hesitate to call this response cognitive. Piaget calls this the "sensory-motor period" of intelligence. But cognitive psychologists, and those like Gagne who attempt to effect a rapprochment between behaviorism and constructivism, consider this period as characterized by associative learning which forms the basis of later logical thinking. Piaget maintains that both operational thought and language use (of the human variety, at least) have their roots in this sensory-motor period and, therefore, could not occur had they not been preceded by the learning that takes place during this period. Both are made possible by the developing ability of the human organism to use symbols to replace objects. The word *danger*, for example, can come to symbolize real danger. It is here that we see most clearly the cognitive basis of language. As Piaget has pointed out, symbolism appears in other forms prior to the emergence of language, most notably in the child's play during this period. He has amply demonstrated both the temporal priority of thinking (as exemplified by the use of symbolism) and the logical priority of thinking in relation to language, and has shown how thought is the natural foundation for the development of language as a human system of communication.

"That is all very well," you may say, "but once language appears on the scene, it develops very rapidly, so that by the time the child is 5 or 6, there is no reason to suppose that one is more important than the other." To the contrary, the meaningful use of language (meaningful to the child, that is) is limited to the extent to which it can be tied in with the child's concrete experiences and developing ability to represent that experience in symbolic terms—of which language is one, painting another, fantasy play yet another.

When we say that language develops rapidly during early childhood or when the linguist tells us that, by age 6, the child's language system contains all the essential features of the adult's, what does this mean? The young child has a vocabulary of approximately 2,500 words at age 6 (Dale, 1972, p. 139), and most of the synthetic structures employed by adults in their spoken language also appear in the child's speech. But this superficial index tells us only that certain words or syntactic structures occur with such-and-such frequency in samples of children's speech. It tells us little about the cognitive events which underlie speech, or which may precede their occurrence.

Although language and thought have common roots in sensory-motor intelligence (as Piaget has maintained), they are thereafter separate but parallel interacting systems. Hence, at any point in an individual's development, language may outstrip thought, or thought may outstrip language. Here, we have to make a distinction between two aspects of meaning, the universal and the individual. The universal aspect includes those characteristics that are essential to the meaning of an utterance and make it possible for us to communicate about something: the denotations of words. The individual aspect includes those characteristics peculiar to a person by virtue of past experience. So, when we compare a child's understanding of words with an adult's, we should keep in mind that the denotative aspects may be perceived differently. Beyond this, the personal meanings attached to words may be profoundly different, partly because of the child's limited perspective on the world and partly because being small, and therefore vulnerable, the child has not yet learned to balance the emotional components that inevitably accompany cognitive learnings.

The business of living is to make sense of the world, to impose a construction on our experience that leads to some kind of order and predictability. We assist the infant in doing this by introducing various forms of regularity and security and by sheltering the baby from frightening or inimical events. As the infant becomes a toddler, stimuli from the environment bombard the senses and language constitutes a major part of this bombardment. Each year, spoken and written words assume an increasing proportion of that part of the surrounding world to which the child is expected to pay attention. Language is symbolic, a "second signal system" as Pavlov called it, and we become awestruck by young children's ability to incorporate this linguistic knowledge into their world consciousness. However, that awe should not prevent us from asking how the child goes about making meaning from linguistic and other kinds of events. Piaget has given us insight into the workings of the child's mind, and others have picked up the torch. But our work is of a different order, including new methods of inquiry and new methods of instruction.

Across the country, a dramatic change is occurring in the attitudes of researchers toward the value of certain types of research which have until now enjoyed only marginal respectability. Naturalistic observation, case studies, interview techniques, and other types of qualitative inquiry have been regarded as suspect because of the degree of subjective interpretation they entail. For 40 years, America has been wedded to the positivistic tradition which posited a value-free social science and applauded methods of inquiry that stressed the objective, empirical, controllable aspects of research. As long ago as the 1950s, Brewster Smith doubted that there could be a value-free psychology and now others are doubting it too. Beyond this question, however, is a further concern about the nature of knowledge and the ecological validity of empiricist methods. To rephrase: If each person's knowledge of the world is constructed from the interplay of mental structures and environmental events, does it not follow that there may be different interpretations of those events? Positivistic methods of inquiry, in order to study a particular phenomenon, abstract it as far as possible from the surrounding environment. Variables that cannot be thus isolated are controlled. Yet, the critics argue that in so doing, positivist researchers pay little attention to the violence that may be done to the phenomenon under investigation. Proponents of empiricist methodologies dismiss this criticism on the grounds that it is the nature of science to be built slowly on ever-accumulating facts that serve as instances of verification or disconfirmation of reigning hypotheses. Despite this dismissal, social scientists, who have long admired and modeled their procedures after those of the physical scientists, are now beginning to look elsewhere for a model. The lead article in *The Chronicle of Higher Education*, March 31, 1980, notes that social scientists, feeling a "serious and widespread uneasiness" over their inability to explain some of the important issues of the day, are groping toward the humanities in an effort to find better explanations. A dominant theme of the 1980 American Educational Research Association annual conference was the "paradigm shift" from the methods of the physical sciences toward those of history, literature, and anthropology. This shift may be viewed as a move away from a preoccupation with group phenomena toward a greater concentration on understanding the individual. In this respect, the newer models may hold greater promise for delivering useful knowledge to educators.

As a parallel development, we may expect to see new methods of instruction that focus attention on individual students. As a consequence of this new ambiance, the language experience approach will enjoy more widespread popularity than before, because it is attuned to the emerging educational philosophies of individualism and rationalism. Let us now examine the ways in which the language experience approach can contribute to the teacher's understanding of the child's cognitive status at a given time.

For Stauffer, one of the leading exponents of this approach, reading *is* thinking: "A process, a dynamic, action-filled way of responding to printed symbols, and not a product of a school subject" (1975, p. 3). Interestingly, he traces this view back to Pestalozzi and Horace Mann. In the 150 years since their work appeared, the view of reading as a cognitive-affective process has recurred in the literature. In 1913, Huey noted that the task of following the author's reasoning, the comprehension and evaluation of facts, and the synthesis of new information to the existing store are "golden practice in the training of judgment" (1913, pp. 363-364). Writing in the 48th Yearbook of the National Society for the Study of Education, Gates went even further.

> To say that reading is a thought-getting process is to give it too restricted a description. It should be developed as a complex organization of patterns of higher mental processes. It can and should embrace all types of thinking, evaluating, judging, imagining, reasoning, and problem-solving. The reader does more than understand and contemplate; his emotions are stirred; his attitudes and purposes are modified; indeed, his innermost being is involved (1949, pp. 3-4).

None of these authors, despite their emphasis on the highest mental processes, neglect the affective dimensions of the reading act. The reader reads for a purpose and is motivated to look for certain kinds of information. In the course of reading, emotions are stirred. As a result of what is read, attitudes are changed. The cognitive and affective, Piaget has remarked, are two banks of the same river. The flow of that river refers to whatever is occurring in a person's brain and body, whether that person is responding to events in the real world or to printed symbols that stand for those events.

Clearly, to conceive of reading as thinking is to emphasize the continuity between the mental operations that have characterized the child's responses to life events in the early years of development and the processes brought into play when the child reads. We hear a good deal about the need to preserve continuity between the child's home language and the language of the school (especially in our reading materials). To my mind, it is more important to preserve cognitive continuity. This means that the concepts and the ideas (not just the language) are familiar, that reading materials are about topics the child finds exciting, and that the values expressed are not alien to those of the child's own culture. As a measure of proficiency is attained, the child can choose what to read, what to identify with, what to internalize.

Viewing reading as thinking also implies a need for individualized instruction. Babies may look alike to the untrained eye, but their genetic equipment at birth is widely different. Once they leave the hospital, their environment is subject to wide ranges of variation. By the time they come to school, children spread across the broad range of every psychological measure of ability, motivation, and learned skill. The teacher's understanding of reading as a thinking process, and his/her willingness to individualize instruction in ways that ensure that every child is challenged are key factors in the successful teaching of beginning reading.

Central to my view of reading as a thinking process is the notion that concept development lies at the heart of the process. This raises the question of what we mean by a concept. In the educational research literature, concept learning is usually regarded as "the identification of concept attributes which can be generalized to newly encountered examples and the discrimination of examples from nonexamples" (Tennyson & Park, 1980, p. 56). Given the large number of concepts students encounter in twelve years of schooling—in science, social studies, math, literature, politics, economics, literature, art, music—perhaps the most we can expect in these terms is that students acquire minimal understanding. Of course, many concepts are explored in depth in the classroom, while the student broadens and enriches some through outside reading and discussion. In fact, the degree to which the student comprehends written material will be a function of previous familiarity with the concepts encountered. Fortunately, reading is a "psycholinguistic guessing game," which means that additional information is picked up during reading. The reader needs prior understanding in order to read but, at the same time, the reading act itself nurtures the cognitive growth of the reader through the process of concept development. Or to put it another way, the *psycho* in *psycholinguistic* is cognitive.

We should not leave this process to chance. We know or suspect that in many families today, where both parents are working and life is pretty much a matter of making ends meet, there is very little discussion or exploration of concepts. We also know that many students do little reading out of school. News of the world comes to them through television commentary (assuming they listen to the news), which of necessity is in capsule form with little in the way of elaboration or explanation. School may be the only place where students acquire more than a superficial understanding of certain concepts. Discussion promotes understanding; after all, adults sharpen their understanding by being presented with new examples and negative instances of a concept, by coming to realize which attributes of the concept are critical and which coincidental.

Young children, Piaget averred, are socialized in their thinking through interaction with other students who are just slightly ahead of them cognitively—not enough to be beyond their grasp, but enough to challenge them in their assertions. I take this statement of Piaget's to have serious implications for instruction. For this reason, I was disturbed by the results of a study reported by Durkin (1978-1979). In surveying classroom practices designed to teach comprehension, Durkin found students spending much time in seatwork activities such as filling in ditto sheets or answers in workbooks. Without denying the value of such exercises, I think we should ask whether some of this time might not be better spent in small group or even class discussions, in which the teacher deliberately provokes exploration of the deeper and fuller meanings of selected concepts. If Durkin is correct in her conclusion that very little is being done to teach comprehension in reading classes, teachers do not have much to lose by using more of the time allocated to reading this way. Small amounts of time invested in this way may have big dividends.

Another implication of this train of thought is that teachers should look beyond minimal criteria to learn if students understand a concept. This in turn suggests a need for informal assessment, perhaps some kind of log-keeping over and above whatever standardized tests or teacher-made tests are used. This log or diary might take the form of jotting down, after a science class, some remark or action that demonstrates a student's lack of understanding or improved understanding of, say, the concept of conservation. At the end of the semester, teachers may be surprised to find how such comments enhance their knowledge of individual students' mastery of the subject matter. On the other hand, they may be disagreeably surprised to find how often they know very little about particular students who are reluctant to expose their ignorance by participating in class discussion. You may object that information acquired through such informal assessment is subjective and unreliable, to which I would respond that students' oral comments may be more revealing of their true understanding than their checkmarks on an objective test, and that most teacher-constructed tests are unreliable anyway.

Before leaving the subject of concepts, it might be well to point out that the term *concept* applies to more than just nouns. We talk about concrete concepts such as *table* and *dog*, or abstract concepts such as *happiness* and *democracy*, or about mathematical concepts such as *equation* and *probability*. These are all nouns. But words like *inside, above, however, equal to, inspite of*, also represent concepts that research shows to be quite difficult to learn. It is true that psychologists are by no means certain of the processes involved in concept learning nor when a concept is comprehended in the course of reading. But we are moving closer to formulating and testing precise hypotheses on these questions. Some theorists (Reder, 1980, p. 22) have suggested that words are analyzed into their semantic primitives during comprehension. A word like *persuade*, would be decomposed into "causes y to intend to do x." To date, there is little evidence either way as to whether such a process actually takes place. Still we are now asking different kinds of questions than we did formerly.

Gagne puts problem solving at the apex of his hierarchy as epitomizing the highest type of mental process; and we are coming to realize more and more that purposive reading requires skills essentially employed in any form of problem solving. Some of the most recent work on comprehension illustrates this point. As a result of the Chomskyian revolution, we went through a decade of preoccupation with the development of understanding of syntax and its role in reading comprehension. Now we have moved to a broader perspective which takes into account the interaction between syntax and semantics, the background of world knowledge that we bring to prose and the presuppositions entailed in that knowledge, as well as the scripts that we as members of a cultural group carry around in our heads ready to be "plugged in" to situations we encounter, including the reading situation. Interest in these topics has increased geometrically, as may be seen from a perusal of dissertation topics submitted for the IRA research award over the past five years. Much of the recent work has grown out of experimental psychology on memory—not unreasonably, if we consider that the object of reading prose (when not purely for distraction) is usually to gain information that we hope to remember. The theory on which much of this research is based revolves around the concept of schema. The authors acknowledge their indebtedness to German philosopher Kant, who may have been the first to use the term, and to British psychologist Bartlett, who conducted several classical studies on memory in the 1930s. However, they fail to mention cognitive psychologist Piaget, who also took the concept from Kant and made it a cornerstone of his epistemological theory. They use the term in very much the same way he does. For example, Rumelhart's definition:

> A schema is a data structure for representing the generic concepts stored in memory. There are schemata representing our knowledge about all concepts: those underlying objects, situations, events, sequences of events, actions and sequences of actions. A schema contains, as part of its specifications, the network of interrelations that is believed to normally hold among the constituents of the concept in question. A schema theory embodies a *prototype* theory of meaning. That is, inasmuch as a schema underlying a concept stored in memory corresponds to the *meaning* of that concept, meanings are encoded in terms of the typical or normal situations or events which instantiate that concept (1981, p. 5).

"Schemata," then, are "truly *the building blocks of cognition.* They are fundamental elements upon which all information processing depends" (p. 4). They are like scripts (Schank & Abelson, 1977) waiting for a particular cast of characters to enact them. They are personal theories about the universe that individuals carry around in their heads. Hence, "the process of understanding discourse is the process of finding a configuration of schemata which offers an adequate account of the passage in question" (p. 26).

You can see what a powerful tool schema theory provides for research on reading comprehension. To date, this research has taken the form of studies on children's comprehension of stories. Do children have a schema in their heads about the way a story should unfold? Do they look for certain components such as situation, character, action, denouement, and do they expect those components to unfold in a certain order? To put it another way, do they have a schema of "plot"? Some of the research suggests that even very young children do have such a schema (Stein & Glenn, 1979).

Another line of research attempting to reveal the cognitive processes underlying reading has been to try to model them and to test the outcome of the modeling process against real data. Many theorists have attempted to represent the structure of prose passages in terms of logical or semantic relations. Some of the earliest work (Dawes, 1964, 1966), like Bartlett's, was concerned with the cognitive distortions that occur in the recall of material read. Bartlett found a tendency for persons to simplify what they had heard and to drop out material that did not fit the overall schema, a tendency he attributed to the process of forgetting. More recent research has been concerned with whether the distortions occur at the point of input when the material is read (in which case the distortion clearly is not a function of forgetting), or whether it occurs at the point of output (in which case the circumstances surrounding recall may influence the kind of distortion that occurs). We have long known that distortions occur at the point where inferences are made. Hence, the nature of inferences has become a focus of attention in some avenues of research into the process (Clark, 1975).

I have tried to demonstrate that reading is a thinking process and that beginning reading, far from being a formal process that is new and alien, should be approached in its continuity with the child's earlier and cognitive structure. Language is important in the process of cognitive development, especially toward the end of the sensory-motor period where the symbolic function begins to evolve. The symbolic function means the capacity to abstract salient and critical features from the perceptual field, the ability to use signs to represent classes of phenomena, and to build hierarchical conceptual systems. Language is an integral part of all these functions, perhaps most importantly in the development of concepts that are the cornerstone of all higher cognitive functions. The language experience approach is based on the postulate that reading is thinking at all levels of the cognitive hierarchy—hence, the cognitive basis of the language experience approach.

Two implications follow. First, to promote thinking is to promote reading. But the connection must be made apparent to children. Everything we do in reading should be designed to promote thinking. The reading lesson is one that calls for the exercise of the teacher's finest creative talents. For this reason, it is disconcerting to find teachers teaching reading in the same ways for the past fifty years. As indicated in various portions of this paper, the most exciting research in reading comprehension taking place today is investigating the psychological processes involved in creating meaning from print. But the ultimate payoff of research can occur only when the results find their way into the classroom. One might expect that at least some teachers would be spearheading such an approach. Yet Durkin's study seems to suggest that only a small portion of reading class time is spent in thinking activities. A more recent observational study by Spiegel and Rogers (1980) investigated teachers' responses to oral reading errors made by second grade children, and classified these responses into eight categories as follows:

1. tell (what the word is);
2. visual (instruct the child to point to the word or look at it again);
3. visual context (the teacher repeats one or two words before the miscue, followed by "what?");

4. sound (child is instructed to sound out the letters);
5. meaning (the teacher shows the anomaly of the erroneous word);
6. structural analysis (the teacher breaks the word into syllables); and
7. reference to prior use (the teacher recalls prior occurrences of the word).

Analysis of the data showed that over 50 percent of all responses fell into the first category (tell), and for all but four of the teachers this was the most frequently used response. A further 29 percent were of the visual, visual context, and spell variety. Only 5 percent of all responses belonged to the meaning category, and about half of these were from one teacher. Perhaps even more distressing than all of the above results was finding that half of the teachers observed showed little variation in their responses to children's errors. No tendency was observed on the part of these teachers to individualize their instruction either to meet different types of errors or different learning styles.

Perhaps the studies by Durkin (1978) and Spiegel and Rogers (in press) report isolated phenomena. We need more such studies to know whether this is the case. As we have noted, naturalistic studies of teaching reading as it occurs in the classroom are coming into their own. This trend will increase. Concurrently, the work on cognitive processes in reading, like the studies derived from schema theory, will proceed. These developments should give us hope that a nationwide plan of instruction based on cognitive considerations will become a phenomenon of the 80s.

References

Clark, H.H. Bridging. In Roger C. Schank and B.L. Nash-Webber (Eds.), *Theoretical issues in natural language processing*. Proceedings of a conference at the Massachusetts Institute of Technology, June 1975.

Dale, P.S. *Language development: Structure and function*. Hinsdale, Illinois: Dryden Press, 1972.

Dawes, R. Cognitive distortion. *Psychological Report*, 1964, *14*, 443-459.

Dawes, R. Memory and the distortion of meaningful written material. *British Journal of Psychology*, 1966, *57*.

Durkin, D. What classroom observations reveal about reading comprehension instruction. *Reading Research Quarterly*, 1978-1979, *14*, 481-533.

Gagne, R.M. *The conditions of learning* (2nd ed.). New York: Holt, Rinehart and Winston, 1970.

Gates, A.I. Character and purposes of the yearbook. In *Reading in the elementary school*, 48th yearbook of the National Society for the Study of Education, Part II. Chicago: University of Chicago Press, 1949.

Huey, E.B. *The psychology and pedagogy of reading*. New York: Macmillan, 1913.

Reder, L.M. The role of elaboration in the comprehension and retention of prose. *Review of Educational Research*, 1980, *50*.

Rumelhart, D.E. Schemata: The building blocks of cognition. In J.T. Guthrie (Ed.), *Comprehension and teaching: Research reviews*. Newark, Delaware: International Reading Association, 1981.

Schank, R.C., & Abelson, R.P. *Scripts, plans, goals, and understanding: An inquiry into human knowledge structures*. Hillsdale, New Jersey: Erlbaum, 1977.

Spiegel, D.L., & Rogers, C. Teacher responses to miscues during oral reading by second grade students. *Journal of Educational Research*, in press.

Stauffer, R.G. *Directing the reading-thinking process*. New York: Harper and Row, 1975.

Stein, N.L., & Glenn, C.C. An analysis of story comprehension in elementary school children. In R.D. Freedle (Ed.), *New directions in discourse processes*. Hillsdale, New Jersey: Erlbaum, 1979.

Tennyson, R.D., & Park, O.C. The teaching of concepts: A review of instructional design research literature. *Review of Educational Research*, 1980, *50*.

Part Two
Beginnings of Literacy:
Talking, Writing, Reading

In the first paper of this section, Parker stresses that language development research in this decade should assume continuity in children's construction of meaning through all forms of language. Too often, he argues, reading, writing, listening, or speaking are isolated for study. This classification problem is reflected both in theory and in research methodology. For example, we can think of them as four separate language processes (listening, speaking, writing, and reading) or as two processes (receptive and expressive) or as one total representational process. Parker recognizes the need to separate processes for analysis, but his emphasis in this paper is on the unity and continuity of the processes. From such a perspective, researchers would look for the early roots of language in nonverbal communication systems, and then toward the individual's development of increasingly complex and more differentiated forms of language.

Children acquire the necessary prerequisites for written language through their own processes of inventing graphic signs and symbols, rather than learning them through direct teaching. While man's historical development of symbol systems supports this view, we may also perceive the teacher as a facilitator in this process. Certainly, the methods used in the more effective British Infant Schools support teachers in such encouragement of children. These are the things Clay (1975) says young writers must do in organizing for themselves a sequence of movements that develop into the writing of a language which can be interpreted by others.

The close connections among linguistic, cognitive, and affective states are supported by Parker's documentation of writing skill regression. In a new or demanding situation in which children's psychological equilibrium is disturbed, a temporary regression often occurs. This usually continues until further cognitive reconstruction results in the mastery of new features which are then incorporated into a new balance of skills. We know temporary regression occurs in other contexts, too. For example, a reflection of disturbed emotional states is frequently found in adult handwriting and spelling; and the graphic activities of drawing and painting often are affected when young children are faced with the social demands of a new or first school situation.

Tough reviews the impact that early language intervention programs are reported to have made on the level of children's literacy. Because such reports indicate little impact, it would seem that the Plowden and Bullock Reports, which stress attention to children with social and intellectual problems, have been either largely ignored or misinterpreted. Despite these discouraging signs, Tough observes the more recent reviews of some of the experimental programs have identified long term benefits. Perhaps the picture is not as dismal as it seems. Tough suggests it is not, and provides a framework for us to look at some instructional components which may lead to greater literacy success for children.

The relationships found between social disadvantage and reading failure among children with no specific mental or emotional handicaps lead Tough to talk about the value of early literary exposure. Because the peripheral factors of familiarity with books and story structure do not fully account for children's reading success, Tough notes that other factors—such as children's understandings of graphic signs and signifiers, perceptual abilities, and the abilities to enter meaning into words—should be carefully studied.

Presenting some of the research growing out of the Communication Skills in Early Childhood Project, which she directs at Leeds University, Tough draws on Sestini's work with young children. A crucial component seems to be the kind of talk children use with others in which they alternately project into others' needs for information and reflect on their own relevant knowledge. Perhaps differences in children's talk at home are related to later reading success. Tough hypothesizes that they are related and that children who have experiences which lead them to a problem-solving orientation may meet reading tasks with less difficulty. Children who are predisposed toward looking for sense in tasks may be more willing to adapt productive problem-solving strategies toward learning to read. Children may, thereby, develop increased abilities to anticipate, predict, or project into the meaning of others—all skills which are basic to reading success.

Looking to oral language development for an understanding of how written language is achieved, Y. Goodman reviews language learning processes. She draws attention to the abilities children acquire to recognize print within, but not out of, context. She notes the similarity of this process of recognition to the early recognition of speech soley within a particular situation. The parallel processes of situation-bound speech and reading and writing give us insight into the similarity of learning processes, regardless of the mode of language.

Identifying the various processes involved in learning language is important because children seem to create their own principles in ways which cannot be taught. The principles develop as children interact with language in appropriate context. Goodman proposes we examine these processes and hypotheses about some of the components which may be involved: functional, the reaction children have to print in context and the effect of parental orientation to reading; linguistic, the organization of written language; and relational, the aspects of written and oral language related to meaning. All become a part of the total language development process.

Each author in this section writes from an interactional, constructive view of language and cognitive development. All stress the need to provide children with rich and varied experiences with reading and writing. It is clear, though, that the way such experiences are presented is important. The authors suggest further examination of the processes involved in children's discovery and refinement of language. Such an examination along with an emphasis on the continuity of learning is imperative as we move toward helping children develop stronger roots for literacy.

Language Development and Learning to Write: Theory and Research Findings[1]

Robert P. Parker
Rutgers University

The way we ask the questions that guide and give direction to our research "limits and disposes" the way in which they may be answered. Thus, our formulation of problems is revealed more fully and tellingly by our questions than by the answers we give to them. Our answers "establish an edifice of facts," but our questions "make the frame in which its picture of facts is plotted" (Langer, 1978). In fact, Langer continues, they

> give the angle of perspective, the palette, the style in which the picture is drawn—everything except the subject. In our questions lie our *principles of analysis*, and our answers may express whatever these principles are able to yield.

With this view in mind, consider the following questions about children's acquisition of written language.

How do children acquire writing? Can we speak of the "onset" of writing? Is there an age, or age span, when children naturally or normally begin to write? Are there demonstrable early stages or phases in the acquisition process? Later stages? Are there patterns of development over time? If so, can these patterns be studied from biological, cognitive, syntactic, semantic, and social points of view? As children acquire writing, can we speak in terms of their evolving linguistic knowledge? Can we apply the competence/performance distinction to writing? Can we talk of children's developing communicative competence in writing?

I have framed these questions about child writing in ways I understand to characterize the guiding questions researchers have posed about the acquisition of spoken language. I have not raised the questions to answer them directly, although I do intend to review the research done to date on acquisition. Rather, by posing questions about child writing in the terms we have used to study child speech, I want to raise a larger question: Can or should we investigate children's writing in the same terms that we have applied to the description and analysis of their talking? If we can use the same terms for both processes and, thus, by extension the same theoretical framework, then perhaps we are studying a single continuous process in development, not two processes. In fact, were we to take that view, we also would have to ask whether listening and reading, as the other major uses of language, should not also be viewed as part of that process. Language acquisition, then, would denote a field of inquiry which includes all four uses of language within its theoretical purview. Within this framework, we could begin our research into writing by assuming, as Vygotsky (1978) does, that "the process of development of written language" is in reality part of "a unified, historical line" which leads from speech, through make-believe play and drawing, to writing.

Actual research practice implies an opposite view. For many child language researchers, language acquisition is synonymous with the acquisition of spoken language. In fact, some use the terms interchangeably. By implication, writing and reading are different, not part of the same continuous process, and therefore not to be studied within the same framework. This isolation of speech research from research on other uses of language has produced two unfortunate results:

1. Until recently, children's acquisition of written language has been ignored, particularly in comparison with the enormous amount of research done on spoken language. Except for Vygotsky, no one has suggested that we need to look beyond spoken language, at other uses of language, in order to understand fully the process of language development. In reality, we may not achieve our fullest understanding of spoken language acquisition until we view language development as a unified,

historical process, thus looking at speaking in relation to listening, writing, and reading.

2. When researchers first began systematic study of children's acquisition of written language, just a few years ago, they seem to have taken their cue from child speech researchers. Most have studied writing by itself, apart from other uses of language, without asking whether the roots of writing lie in earlier processes which may provide precursors or prerequisites for its development.[2] Nor does there seem to be an explicit sense that writing may, in turn, serve as a precursor of language (or other) development still to come.

As a first point in my theoretical picture, I propose that writing development be viewed as a part of a continuous process of language development—including, respectively, listening, talking, writing, and reading—and that the process overall be approached as unitary and historical. In fact, given the recent work on prespeech communication by Bruner (1975a, 1975b, 1978) and others (Dore, 1978; Snow, 1978; Sugarman, 1973), certains forms of prespeech interaction between infants and mothers (or other primary caretakers) appear to serve as the basis for the development of communicative functions which, in turn, provide "the matrix for the acquisition of language" (Bruner, 1978). Bruner has discussed four of these communicative functions in detail: "1) the inference of communicative intent, 2) the nature of early reference, 3) the use of language in the regulation of joint action, and 4) the precursors of predication" (1975). The development of these functions, he emphasizes, arises from constant mother-child interactions in situations whose formats become regularized and ritualized. Within these recurring formats, children slowly and steadily learn how to communicate intentionally and meaningfully, i.e., they achieve increasing communicative competence, and this process provides a clear line of continuity in "the transition from prelinguistic to linguistic communication."

As Halliday (1975, 1976) has so trenchantly pointed out, throughout this entire process the child is learning how to mean. So it is not simply or strictly a linguistic process that we are witnessing but a semiotic process: a process of development in meaning-making which begins before the onset of spoken language and which, increasingly, is realized through the use of linguistic and other symbols. Here is the way Halliday (1975) puts it:

> A child who is learning his first language is learning how to mean; in this perspective, the linguistic system is to be seen as a semantic potential. It is a range of possible meanings, together with the means whereby these meanings are realized or expressed.

And further,

> It is our contention that the learning of language is essentially the learning of a semantic system, and that this process is already well under way before the child has any words at all. He learns to mean long before he adopts the lexical mode for the realization of meanings.

Piaget also stressed the importance of the process of development in the representational or semiotic function. In his view, this is the overarching process and language takes a place in its evolution, along with other symbolic modes. Following Saussure, Piaget defined the semiotic function as "the ability to represent something (a signified something: object, event, conceptual scheme, etc.) by means of a 'signifier' which is differentiated and which serves only a representative purpose: language, mental image, symbolic gesture and so on" (Piaget & Inhelder, 1969). Piaget also emphasized "the *common* manifestations of the semiotic function and...the *continuity* between sensorimotor action schemes and verbal schemes" (Karmiloff-Smith, 1979). Thus, like Bruner, he saw in organized prelinguistic schemes of action the precursors of verbal language as well as the prerequisites for the whole of symbolic development.

Karmiloff-Smith (1979) notes, however, that Piaget studied exclusively children's interactions with the world of objects. Bruner, on the other hand, has focused on children's interactions with the world of persons, especially primary caretakers. His concern has been children's social world rather than their physical world. In an effort to make the research picture complete, Karmiloff-Smith examined children's interaction with language as "a crucial problem area for the child in his own right" (1979). As a result, we now have evidence of the contribution to language development in particular, and semiotic development in general, made by children's interactions with objects, language, and people.

Halliday provides the final and, in some respects, most crucial piece in this theoretical picture. Language, he notes,

> is only one way of exchanging meanings with others, even though it may be in some sense the most important one. The whole of our culture is an edifice of meanings, and we cannot help exchanging meanings with other people by the way we act and interact...the whole set of semiotic processes that make up the life of a community. I have sometimes referred to this mode of interpretation as "sociosemiotic," to take account of the fact that learning to mean linguistically is just one aspect of learning to mean as a social process (1976, 12-13).

In summary, I am urging a theoretical view of writing development as a process which is itself both continuous with, and embedded in, three broader processes, each related but each overarching and encompassing the others. First, writing development is part of an ongoing process of language development, which has its roots in the prespeech communication of mothers and infants and continues on through listening, talking, writing, and reading. Second, language development is itself part of a broader process of semiotic development, which includes gesture, make-believe play, drawing, and dance. Third, semiotic development is part of a still broader social process which involves the creation and transmission of cultural as well as individual meanings.

Within this sociosemiotic framework, it seems most appropriate to approach the analysis of semiotic development generally, and language development particularly, from the explicit interactionist-constructivist perspective which Piaget has adopted and which he and other cognitive psychologists have argued is the best alternative to nativist and empiricist viewpoints.

As Langer has noted, an interest in symbols and symbolic processes arose early in this century. This concern with symbolization, she argues, met new problems in the theory of knowledge and thus inspired "an evaluation of science and a quest for certainty." It led also, she claims, "in the opposite direction—to psychiatry: The study of emotions, religion, fantasy, and everything but knowledge." There is, however, a central theme which runs through these diverse lines of inquiry: "The *human response*, as a constructive, not a passive thing." From this concern with human symbolization has come a new conception of mind, and mental functioning, which we can see in such diverse sources as in the transactionalist philosophy of Dewey, the constructivist epistemology of Piaget, and the personal construct psychology of Kelly (1955).

In *Genetic Epistemology* (1971: 15) Piaget provides one of the clearest expositions of this perspective:

> I think that human knowledge is essentially active. To know is to assimilate reality into systems of transformations. To know is to transform reality in order to understand how a certain state is brought about. By virtue of this point of view, I find myself opposed to the view of knowledge as a copy, a passive copy of reality. In point of fact, this notion is based on a vicious circle: in order to make a copy we have to know the model that we are copying, but according to this theory of knowledge the only way to know the model is by copying it. . . . To my way of thinking, knowing an object does not mean copying it—it means acting upon it. It means constructing systems of transformations that can be carried out on or with this object. Knowing reality means constructing systems of transformations that correspond, more or less adequately, to reality. They are more or less isomorphic to transformations of reality. The transformational structures of which knowledge consists are not copies of the transformations in reality; they are simply possible isomorphic models among which experience can enable us to choose. Knowledge, then, is a system of transformations that become progressively adequate.

Looked at from this perspective, the child's process of learning how to mean, and of doing so increasingly through linguistic means, seems to me to be most generally and consistently characterized by the quality of construction or invention. Through this process, and during the phases concerned with development in the various meaning systems (gesture, words, play, drawing, writing), the child seems to be constantly constructing and reconstructing, or inventing and reinventing, ways to participate with others in the social process of making and sharing meanings.

Some years ago, Bruner (1972) put the proposition this way:

> The child, exposed linguistically to an adult world, comes forth not with a discovery but with an invention...in a linguistic form that simply is not present in the adult repertoire. Such language learning consists of invention or coming forth with grammar.

A few years later, Halliday (1975) presented a similar though more elaborated characterization of the process. The child, he said,

> is constructing a semantic system, and this implies...that he is also at the same time constructing a lexicogrammatical and phonological system as the way of "realizing" his meaning potential. He begins (if my observations are at all typical) by inventing a semantics of his own, a "proto-language" that is not a form of the mother tongue and that consists only of content and expression....Then he moves into the mother tongue, and the system becomes a three-level one consisting of meaning, wording, and sound.

Building up this system for realizing meanings is a social process, and one to which the child makes a crucial contribution.

> What the child does, I think, is to create a language and a reality in partnership with others; they are working at it together. And it is the child who is providing the driving force. The mother, and other important people, do the steering—though the child always struggles to get his hand on the wheel, too (Halliday, 1976).

Bruner uses the term *invention* to characterize the child's contribution to this process, and Halliday speaks alternatively of the child's constructing, inventing, and creating the means for realizing meaning. In fact, semiotic development involves a constant process of invention and reinvention. The prelinguistic infant invents and reinvents communicative gestures which gradually become more like adult gestures and, therefore, more meaningful to a wider variety of people. The same overall process is true for speech. Children's first "words" are invented, a "proto-language" which has meaning only to one or two primary caretakers. Gradually, children revise their constructions (linguistic forms) in order to make more sense of the adult utterances they encounter. Through this process, children invent the constructions that motivate the adult's linguistic behavior. In so doing, children move their utterances closer and closer to adult forms; in Piaget's terms, their symbols become progressively adequate in predicting what adults will say. And the same is true for children's syntax. They invent their own unique word combinations and word order, and then transform them. Eventually, they come to resemble adult syntax more closely.

Children's symbolic play presents a similar picture, as does their drawing. At first, their play is idiosyncratic; its symbolic value (or meaning) is implicit, available only to an intimate few. Gradually, however, children reconstruct their play sequences, making the meaning of them more readily and widely available. Over time, children's symbolic play becomes more broadly and effectively communicative, particularly toward the beginning of play sequences, as they name certain objects or actions as being something else: as they more intentionally and consciously create and use symbolic meanings.

A similar evolution occurs in children's drawings. At first, children are unaware of the symbolic meanings of their drawings, and at first their drawings may be invented versions of things which are not generally recognizable and, therefore, not meaningful to others. Gradually, however, as with symbolic play, children construct graphic depictions which become more like real objects. Simultaneously, they discover that their graphic representation is not another actual object, but a symbol of that object. Moreover, the ability to engage in this process—this series of successive transformations of reality in drawing—is made possible by speech. In Vygotsky's words:

> We feel...most justified in asserting that primary symbolic representation should be ascribed to speech, and that it is on the basis of speech that all other sign systems are created (1978).

And further, referring to a series of experiments in which children were given the task of graphically depicting some more or less complex verbal phrase:

> we see how drawing obediently follows the phrase and how spoken language intrudes into children's drawings. In this process, the children frequently had to make genuine discoveries in inventing an appropriate mode of representation, and we were able to see that this is decisive in the development of writing and drawing in children (1978).

What does the picture look like for writing? What does the modest amount of research, and the even more modest amount of theory, look like in the light of the broad theoretical picture I have been sketching?

Generally, when children first attempt to "write" whether on command or at their own initiation, their writing, like their drawing, consists of "meaningless and undifferentiated squiggles and lines" (Vygotsky, 1978). Often the children themselves cannot "read" their writings; that is, they cannot say what the writing means. Other times they can—and in full detail. These first writings are

> *gross approximations* which later become refined: weird letter forms, invented words, make-believe sentences. Such creative efforts suggest that the child is reaching out toward the principles of written language (Clay, 1979).

Children making their first attempts at writing seem to have a general idea of what writing is, although that idea lacks differentiation and accurate detail. From this idea, children proceed to invent, and reinvent, how to write—teaching themselves how to write in ways that move from the "gross approximations" Clay notes to more specific, more accurate, more highly differentiated, more socially appropriate, and more meaningful approximations.

Clay's work (1979) provides support for this characterization of early writing development both as inventive and as moving from a crude wholistic view of the activity to a mastery of the different parts of the activity. Clay says:

> The individual child's progress in mastering the complexity of the writing system seems to involve letters, words, and word groups *all at one time*, at first in *approximate*. . .and what seem to be *primitive* ways and later with considerable skill. (See also Luria, 1977-1978; Wiseman & Watson, 1980.)

Intially, children's writing is not writing at all, but undifferentiated scrawling which has no functional significance. Luria (1977-1978) called this phase of nonfunctional scribbling "preinstrumental," describing the child's understanding of writing thus:

> Although the child at this stage does not yet grasp the sense and function of writing, he...tries to reproduce, if only in its outward form, adult writing with which he is familiar.

Occasionally, however, children's writing serves a mnemonic function. Though the writing remains "undifferentiated in its outward appearance," it is "transformed into a memory-helping sign." From this point, the child slowly reconstructs these "primary graphic signs" as true "symbolic signs" which express a "specific content."

Broadly viewed, children's writing development is marked by a movement from the production of crude, primitive syncretistic wholes toward increasingly differentiated, multiskilled, detailed wholes. Based on earlier linguistic (and other semiotic) achievements, plus whatever experience they have of written language itself, children initially construct primitive, unskilled approximations of writing, meaningful only to intimates who assume them to be so. Slowly, these crude approximations are transformed and the child develops communicative competence in the new mode. And, so Luria (1977-1978) notes:

> Development...may be marked by a gradual improvement in the process of writing within the means of each technique, with sharp turning points marking a transition from one such technique to another. But the profound dialectical uniqueness of this process means that the transition to a new technique sets the process of writing back considerably after which it develops further at the new and higher level.

Though Clay (1979), unlike Luria, found no evidence of stages in the early writing development of children (from ages 4:10 to 7:00), she did describe a number of interesting features of early child writing,[3] some of which support Luria's broad theoretical outline. As a matter of learning to write, she found, children must learn

- to understand that print talks
- to form letters
- to build up memories of common words they can construct out of letters
- to use those words to write messages
- to increase the number and range of sentences
- to discipline the expression of ideas within the spelling and punctuation conventions of English (1977).

This list does not represent a sequence of (or for) these learnings, nor in fact can children readily or usefully be taught to do these things in this or in any other sequence. As Clay notes, children "learn faster if they are able to organize for themselves a sequence of movements"; that is, if they are allowed to teach themselves, through trial and error, the movements required to make, for example, "one or two letter forms, this also seems to teach /them/ how to organize /their/ approach to new forms."

In addition to her delineation of these features of early child writing, Clay also identified two principles which seem to underlie most children's spontaneous writing activity. She found many children spontaneously repeating certain forms (the *recurring* principle) and varying certain forms (the *flexibility* principle). Though being asked, or required, to copy contributed little to their writing development, spontaneous copying or repetition appeared to be quite beneficial. Even more beneficial, it seemed, was the children's spontaneous creation of "contrasts in visual form, letters, meaning, and sounds." The children Clay studied regularly displayed an urge to take inventory of their accomplishments: a "need to take stock, a need to reorder known items, perhaps to group, and then to regroup in different ways...."

Left to themselves, her subjects experimented with letter forms, creating "a variety of new symbols by repositioning or decorating the standard forms." This experimentation enabled them "to explore the limits within which each letter form might be varied and still retain its identity." It enabled them to begin to answer the question: "When is a sign a new sign?" Clay concludes, many of the "errors" children make in their creative writing at this early point in their development "must be regarded as indicators of this flexibility which is essential for the complex learning to be mastered," and not as indicators of deficiencies in knowledge or skill.

And, as Clay and Luria have found, when children are faced with a new dimension of writing to be mastered, or when they are exploring the limits of this new feature, "responses which are already adequate may recover their flexibility and letters or words may reappear in wrong positions, wrong forms, and wrong orders. Thus new difficulties or problems in the writing situation can produce a regression in recently learned responses" (Graves, 1979b).

This regression is clearly illustrated by the case of Andrea, age 8, one of the children studied in detail by Graves and his coworkers in their two-year study of the writing development of children aged 6-10 (Graves, 1979b, 1979c). For the first month of school Andrea wrote regularly, easily, and quickly (an average 15.5 words per minute).

> Her stories were well developed with good characters and complex sequences of action. Furthermore, she was a good critic of other writings (1979b, p. 317).

Yet, she seldom revised her own writing, and then only at the word unit level. In Graves' words, "Andrea's development as a writer had reached a plateau" (1979b). Then, in mid-October, the teacher asked Andrea and other children to write about a personal experience. She also asked them to write three different "leads" (or beginnings) before completing the piece. As Andrea wrote the leads, her writing suddenly became temporary, a first draft, not permanent, and she approached it in a new way. What she wrote did not have to be perfect the first time; it could be revised later and made perfect then. As one result, her handwriting changed from her "usual clean square letters" to a "loose, loopy scrawl." This happens, Graves notes, for "most children: When a child tries a new approach to writing, other areas suffer temporarily" (1979c, p. 573).

This same kind of regression occurred for Sarah, another child in Graves' research, and for Anne and Julie, the two first graders studied by Donnelly and Stevens (1980). Sowers (1979) offers this summary of Sarah's writing:

> When Sarah attempts a new step in writing, the burden may alter her syntax, penmanship, spelling or any other recently learned features of her writing. They will no longer be automatic.

There is, it seems, a delicate balance among the features of writing that the child has "mastered" at any given point in her early development. When she directs her energy and attention toward the task of constructing competence in a new feature of writing, like revision beyond the word unit level, this balance is disturbed and a temporary regression in "skill" occurs. Eventually she effects a further reconstruction, with the new feature now incorporated to create a new cluster or system of features which have been mastered—and, thus, a new balance of "skills."

Children's free spelling is the feature of child writing which has been most directly and explicitly characterized as inventive, and most completely described from that perspective. Read's work (1971, 1976) presents the fullest documentation of invented spellings as a widespread and interesting phenomenon, although others (Chomsky, 1971, 1975, 1976; Donnelly & Stevens, 1980; Klein & Schickedanz, 1980; Paul, 1976) have commented on it also, and Graves and his associates investigated it as part of their longitudinal research (Calkins, 1979; Graves, 1979b).

Read found that children as young as 3½ years began inventing spellings of words, often arranging movable letters or letter-like objects before they had the coordination to manipulate a pencil or crayon. Many of these children continued to invent spellings or words long after they had learned to read standard spelling, though "the characteristics of the invented spelling did change...under the influences of standard spelling" (1976). Significantly, none of the children encountered difficulty in learning to use standard spelling, a finding others have corroborated (Graves, 1979; Parker, in progress). Read regards the invented spellings

> as based on a set of tacit hypotheses about phonetic relationships and sound spelling correspondences, which the child was able to modify readily as he or she encountered new information about standard spelling (1976).

The parents' responses to their children's spelling efforts were significant. Though some seemed "surprised and puzzled" by the productions, and a few "worried about the development of bad spelling," all of them accepted the invented spellings as "creative productions" and "offered adult spelling only when the child asked for it."

So far, I have discussed the findings of research on child writing. In the one attempt so far to propose a theory of early writing development (King & Rentel, 1979), the authors argue (though not as a central tenet of their theory) that "children learn how to write as a natural extension of their desire to communicate both to themselves and others." In this process, children "hypothesize, discover, invent, correct, and approximate the distinctive conventions of writing." Unfortunately, they neither view writing development in the broader context of language development, nor view language development as part of the still broader process of sociosemiotic development. As a result, they fail to develop the theoretical implications of these assertions about child writing. Why, for example, children hypothesize, discover, invent, and approximate writing is simply ignored. They do, however, review two areas of child knowledge which seem related to writing development. Following Britton (1970) and Moffett (1968), they note that children's ability to sustain discourse on a topic "appears to predict a necessary representational prelude to writing ability."

Also, they examine what is known about children's sense of story, particularly children's knowledge of "certain story conventions and narrative structures." As they note, various researchers (Applebee, 1978, 1977) report a clear developmental progression in children's story knowledge, as evidenced in their telling and retelling of stories, and characterize this progression most commonly as a process of "schematization"—or of developing internal representations of what stories are. Again, however, the lack of an explicit a priori theoretical framework, prevents a full explanation of why these areas of knowledge might contribute to writing development or how this contribution might be made.

As I suggested earlier, a fruitful theoretical framework for the analysis of child writing would include the following assumptions about learning and development, at least as far as language is concerned.

1. Language development would be viewed as a unitary process, consisting of four main uses: listening, speaking, writing, and reading. Development in one use would be viewed against the individual's overall history of development in the various uses, with the retrospect of earlier uses and the prospect of later uses always in mind.

2. The process of language development would be viewed as a part of a broader process of semiotic development, itself unitary, and again with the individual's history of development in meaning-making (past and anticipated) as the backdrop for any analysis.

3. Individual semiotic development would be viewed as part of a broader sociosemiotic process, also unitary and again forming part of the backdrop for analysis of any of the hypothetically constituent parts.

4. Finally, at least for my purposes here, learning and development per se would be viewed from an interactionist-constructivist perspective. Individuals, it would be assumed, actively construct knowledge for themselves through their interactions with the events of their environment, including inner mental processes as well as physical objects, people, symbol systems, and social processes. In this regard, knowledge of and about language would be constructed and reconstructed—or invented and reinvented—just as is knowledge of anything else in the person's experience.

When the facts of child writing, as the scanty research presents them, are considered in the light of this theory (however skeletal) they appear to make sense. That is, this theory appears to provide a fruitful perspective for viewing child writing (in its developmental course), at least in light of the evidence currently available. The history of child writing development, as Luria described it, does seem to involve "a whole series of little inventions and discoveries" within the confines of each technique, punctuated by the "sharp turning points" which mark major transformations or reconstructions of those techniques so that the entire process, after that, proceeds on a "new and higher level." Perhaps the facts of development in listening, speaking, and reading may look different, and more coherent, when they are viewed from within this framework.

Footnotes

[1]Two of my colleagues, Wallis Reid and Marjorie Arnold, offered helpful comments on this article and I have incorporated their criticisms and suggestions.

[2]The one exception is the article by King and Rentel (1979).

[3]Donnelly and Stevens (1980) didn't find any evidence of stages in the writing development of the two 6 year olds they studied.

References

Bruner, J.S. From communication to language: A psychological perspective. *Cognition*, 1975, *3*, 255-287. Also in S. Markova (Ed.), *The social context of language*. New York: John Wiley, 1978.

Bruner, J.S. Learning how to do things with words. In J.S. Bruner and A. Garton (Eds.), *Human growth and development*. Oxford: Oxford University Press, 1978.

Bruner, J.S. The ontogenesis of speech acts. *Journal of Child Language*, 1975, *2*, 1-19.

Calkins, L. Children learn the writers craft. *Language Arts*, 1980, *57*.

Calkins, L. Punctuate! punctuate? punctuate. *Learning Magazine*, 1980.

Calkins, L. Research update: Andrea learns to make writing hard. *Language Arts*, 1979, *57*, 569-576.

Chomsky, C. How sister got into the grog. *Early Years*, 1975, *6*.

Clay, M.M. *What did I write?* Auckland, New Zealand: Heinemann Educational Books, 1975. (United States Edition, 1979.)

deVilliers, P.A., & deVilliers, J.G. *Early language.* Cambridge, Massachusetts: Harvard University Press, 1979.

Donnelly, C., & Stevens, G. Streams and puddles: A comparison of two young writers. *Language Arts*, 1980, 735-741.

Durkin, D. *Children who read early*. New York: Teachers College Press, 1966.

Graves, D. Research update: A new look at writing research. *Language Arts*, 1980, *58*, 913-919.

Graves, D. Research update: Research doesn't have to be boring. *Language Arts*, 1979, *57*, 76-80.

Graves, D. Research update: What children show us about revision. *Language Arts*, 1979, *57*, 312-317.

Graves D. Research update. Writing research for the eighties: What is needed. *Language Arts*, 1981, *58*.

Hall, M., Moretz, S., & Staton, J. Writing before grade one: A study of early writers. *Language Arts*, 1976, 582-585.

Halliday, M.A.K. How children learn language. Mimeographed, 1976.

Halliday, M.A.K. *Learning how to mean: Explorations in the development of language.* London: Edward Arnold, 1975.

Kamler, B. Research update. One child, one teacher, one classroom: The story of one piece of writing. *Language Arts*, 1980, 680-693.

Karmiloff-Smith, A. *A functional approach to child language*. New York: Cambridge University Press, 1979.

King, M., & Rentel, V. Toward a theory of early writing development. *Research in the Teaching of English*, 1979, *13*, 243-253.

Klein, A., & Schickedanz, J. Preschoolers write messages and receive their favorite books. *Language Arts*, 1980, *58*, 742-749.

Kroll, B., Kroll, D.L., & Wells, C.G. Researching children's writing development: The children learning to write project. *Language for Learning*, 1980, *2*.

Paul, R. Invented spelling in kindergarten. *Young Children*, 1976, *31*.

Petty, W.T. The writing of young children. In C.R. Cooper and L. Odell (Eds.), *Research on composing*. Urbana, Illinois: National Council of Teachers of English, 1978.

Piaget, J. *Genetic epistemology*. New York: W.W. Norton, 1971.

Piaget, J., & Inhelder, B. *The psychology of the child*. New York: Basic Books, 1969.

Read, C. *Children's categorization of speech sounds in English*. Urbana, Illinois: National Council of Teachers of English, 1976.

Snow, C. The development of conversation between mothers and babies. *Journal of Child Language*, 1977, *4*, 1-22.

Snow, C., & Ferguson, C. (Eds.). *Talking to children*. Cambridge, England: Cambridge University Press, 1977.

Sowers, S. Research update. A six-year-old's writing process: The first half of first grade. *Language Arts*, 1979, *57*, 829-835.

Sugarman-Bell, S. Some organizational aspects of prelinguistic communication. In I. Markova (Ed.), *The social context of language*. New York: John Wiley and Sons, 1978.

Vygotsky, L.S. *Mind in society: The development of higher psychological processes*. Cambridge, Massachusetts: Harvard University Press, 1978.

Wiseman, D., & Watson, D. The good news about becoming a writer. *Language Arts*, 1980, *58*, 750-755.

Children's Use of Language and Learning to Read

Joan Tough
Univesity of Leeds

During recent years in Britain (as elsewhere) there has been considerable criticism of what are now referred to as progressive methods of teaching. Claims of a fall in standards of literacy and numeracy have frequently cited progressive methods as the cause. These claims have had their effect on teachers, discouraging those who were trying to develop child-centered discovery methods, and encouraging those who had resisted change.

The development of so called progressive methods was given impetus by the Plowden Report (HMSO, 1967). This report made recommendations about ways in which primary education might contribute more to solving the problems of educational disadvantage. It supported the view that learning would be improved by teaching methods that focused on the needs of individual children and by a "discovery approach" that would not only motivate children through greater involvement in their own learning but at the same time place learning on a sounder conceptual basis. The recommendations also included providing increased educational resources in areas of social disadvantage. Criticisms mounted as years went by and it became clear that the problems had not disappeared as the result of new measures and approaches.

Recently, however, research has revealed that there is no justification for claims that standards of literacy have fallen. Not only is there no evidence to support that view, but progressive methods of teaching are found to be something of a myth. In 1976, research into teaching styles and pupil progress found that only one in six teachers was using progressive methods (Bennett, 1976). Such a proportion could hardly account for the claimed fall in standards. Moreover, an official survey of primary schools found that the majority of teachers in the survey were using traditional methods, or a mixture of traditional and progressive methods, with few relying entirely on progressive methods (HMSO, 1978). More recent research into classroom practice in primary schools has found that, generally, design and organization of classrooms which were evolved to support progressive teaching methods by increasing the possibilities for interaction between teachers and children, and for activities in small groups, have now become convenient ways of deploying children to use individual assignments which require little initiative on the part of children, involve little interaction between teachers and children, and do not promote cooperative investigation in small groups (Galton, Simon, & Croll, 1980). It seems from this that much of what the Plowden Report recommended has either been ignored or misinterpreted, and many teachers have taken refuge in graded exercises as the safest way of providing for individual needs.

But if these studies show that standards of literacy are being maintained, they also show that we have made little headway in overcoming the problems of educational disadvantage and underachievement. A major recommendation of the Plowden Report was that there should be an expansion of educational provisions for children between the ages of 3 and 5 years, particularly in areas of social disadvantage. There was some disillusionment when the benefits from preschool education were not shown to be immediate and clear and the program was not fully implemented and has suffered under recent cuts in spending on education. But as in the case of Head Start programs, a recent evaluation of some experimental preschool programs has shown that there have been some long term gains for children (Lazar & Darlington, 1978).

The importance of preschool and early school years was reemphasized in the Bullock Report (HMSO, 1975). This report recognized the need for teachers to reconsider the role of language in learning at all ages, and in all areas of the curriculum, and focused on the early years as the period of great potential for the development of language, and for laying the foundations for reading.

The importance of early experiences through which children learn to use language is now widely recognized. Studies have drawn attention to the disadvantage many school children experience from language used in their homes. Although Bernstein's work has received considerable criticism, few would deny the stimulus his early work gave to research in this area or that the link between social class and educational achievement is explained, in part, by the way in which language mediates meanings at the levels of concepts, attitudes, and expectations (Bernstein, 1971). Achievement in education clearly depends upon skills of reading and writing which, at later stages of education, must draw extensively on children's abilities to use language in comprehending texts, searching for information in books, and displaying knowledge and understanding through writing.

In the early stages of reading, the relationship is not so clear. Language used in first books may be unfamiliar to children but generally it is not so complex, either in meaning or in structure, as the language children use in conversation. During recent years there have been attempts to use familiar language, to base reading on content that appeals to readers of all ages and from different social backgrounds, and to use the children's own language in first reading books. There is an awareness that children can be alienated from reading and books by content with which they cannot identify. This does not mean that all children now use books which in all ways support their induction into the reading process, but the need for this is well understood.

There is considerable difference between children in the age at which they begin to read and in the rapidity of progress once they have started. Early readers are not necessarily better readers by the age of 8 than those who start to read later. But those children who do not start to read before 7½ are likely to have persistent problems (Clark, 1970; Morris, 1966). Further, we know that reading problems are more widespread among the socially disadvantaged (Davie et al., 1972; Little et al., 1972; Morris, 1959).

Why should some children who are of normal intelligence and who apparently have no specific handicaps fail to begin to read when they meet appropriate teaching, and why should the problem be associated with social disadvantage? Failure to read is often explained by lack of motivation, lack of parental interest, and, more recently, by children's experiences with language used in their homes.

There have been some attempts to examine the relationships between children's experiences at home and their success in learning to read. In particular, the value of parents reading stories to children has been investigated. Donachy (1979) reported on recent work in Scotland in which parents were encouraged to read books regularly to their children. These children were more successful in learning to read than those whose parents had not taken part in the project. Early work by Durkin (1966) showed that children who began to read early, and without formal instruction, had experiences of stories read to them by parents. Margaret Clark (1976) investigated the early experiences of children who were already reading fluently when they came to school. In no case had reading been taught formally but all the children had regular experiences of stories being read by parents.

The reasons put forward for the association between experience of hearing stories read and of successful initiation into reading include children's greater familiarity with the language of books; the development of the concept of "story"; the establishment of book skills, including familiarity with the direction in which pages turn and the top to bottom, left to right orientation of print; and the view that print holds meanings which can be extracted by those who know how. In addition, children learn the value set on books and on reading and they learn to expect that they will soon have the pleasure of reading for themselves.

Such experiences are important but it seems unlikely that they account fully for success in learning to read, for many other skills are involved. To read successfully, children must recognize that graphic signs stand for spoken language; they must distinguish between letter shapes and see significance in the arrangement of letters in words; and they must be oriented to search for small but significant features in shape and order of letters and associate these with vocal sounds and spoken words. More than this, children must enter into the meaning of the words they read in sequence, projecting through the imagination into the meanings. This is a difficult task and, to succeed, children must look for clues to help; they must use their knowledge of language and predict the words that are likely to follow.

To learn to read successfully, then, children need skills of observing and analyzing at both visual and auditory levels. They also need reasoning and problem solving attitudes and a readiness to predict and imagine. Is there any evidence to support the view that children need these skills if they are to deal successfully with experiences of learning to read?

Some evidence emerged from a longitudinal study of the development of language between the ages of 3 and 7½ years (Tough, 1977). In this study, the language of two groups of twenty-four children from different social environments was recorded in a variety of situations at ages 3, 5½, and 7½. The parents of one group of children had the minimum period of education and were unskilled or semiskilled manual workers, and one or both parents of a second group of children had received higher education and worked in a profession or occupation of comparable status. At the same time of selection, at age 3, all the children were friendly and talking clearly, all were well cared for, and were of average intelligence or above. The mean IQ of the two groups was about the same at the age of 3½. From the analysis of the language data the following facts emerged.

On all measures of complexity of linguistic structure—including utterance length, the use of clauses, the complexity of the noun phrase, and the verb phrase—children of educationally advantaged parents scored significantly higher than children of educationally disadvantaged parents. However, when the range of complexity of these was examined, the differences were found to be less. All children used complex structures but the children of educationally disadvantaged parents used them less frequently than the other group.

When the purposes for which the children used language were examined, it was found that children of parents with educational advantages more frequently used language to analyze and reflect on present and past experiences; to reason and justify; to predict and consider alternative possibilities; to talk about events in the future; to project into the lives and feelings of others; and to build up scenes, events, and stories in the imagination.

The study concluded that all the children studied had experienced language from which they had established similar knowledge about the language system. They had different orientations toward the use of language, however, which accounted not only for the different purposes for which they chose to use language but also for the differences in mean scores on measures of linguistic complexity. For significant differences of this kind to emerge it seemed that children must have had experiences that differed widely, and attempts were made to discover something of the nature of those experiences.

Research into differences in mother-child interaction has not been extensive. Hess and Shipman's study (1965) is almost unique in examining talk between children and their mothers from different social backgrounds as the mothers taught the children how to carry out a simple task. The results suggesting that children were being socialized into different cognitive modes are well known.

Halliday's (1975) studies of parent-child interaction show how early holophrases gradually emerge into differentiated grammatical elements. Studies by Snow have shown that, on the whole, parents provide a well formed model from which children learn language, but they tend to reduce the complexity of their utterances when talking with young children (Snow & Ferguson, 1977; Snow, 1979).

A major project by Wells (1979) attempted to follow over several years the informal conversations of mothers and children at home. The study used the automatic recording of 90 second examples of children's talk every 20 minutes spread over a day. This has provided a unique collection of data from which the sequence of language development in relation to children's experience of talk with parents can be plotted. However, 90 second samples cannot provide evidence of the build up of discussion and the elaboration of ideas that develop through a number of exchanges, and it seems unlikely that the data will be entirely representative of children's experiences or skills. Wells' study shows that even families of similar social background differ considerably in what he refers to as "the reciprocal negotiations of meaning."

Among studies of language in the home there is some reference to reading books. For example, Bakher-Renes and Hoefnaghe-Hohle (1974) showed that mothers' speech was more complex in free situations which included playing, chatting after a meal, and reading a book. It was found that the most complex use of language occurred when reading books. Snow and associates also found that reading books stimulated the most complex speech (Snow et al., 1976). Several studies have examined the effects of reading stories on children's growth of vocabulary, or producing more complex adult-child interaction (Ackerman, 1976; Irwin, 1960; Mitner, 1951). While children become familiar with books during such activities, it may be that the predominant benefit is due to the stimulation given to language development by children's attempts to deal with complex ideas through talk with adults.

As part of the longitudinal study of children's use of language, an attempt was made to discover something of the nature of children's experiences at home. Although some recordings were made of talk between mothers and children, this was not feasible for all. Elizabeth Sestini carried out a structured interview with each mother when the children were 7½. The interview was devised to produce evidence of mothers' views of children studied and the kind of talk and activity they shared, including the mothers' methods of control, their views of education and of their children's progress in school, and of their hopes for their children's future. The mothers' responses in the interviews also provided evidence of the mothers' way of thinking and of expressing ideas in talk (Sestini, 1975).

Analysis of this data produced interesting insights into different ways mothers viewed their children, relationships between mothers and their children, the expectations conveyed to the children, the different characteristics of their thinking, and of the experience the children would have in hearing their mothers talk with other adults. It also gave insight into the kind of interaction that took place between members of the family and the topics around which talk revolved.

The Nature of Adult-Child Dialogue

How important is the talk with adults in which children are frequently involved? Language is a means of communicating meanings, but there are problems in communicating with children through the use of language when not only their skill in using language is immature but their meanings are also underdeveloped and immature and, perhaps, unrecognized by children themselves.

Young children are unable to project into another's point of view and need help in escaping from their own egocentricity. When children talk with adults there is a gulf between their meanings which only the adults can appreciate. This gulf can be bridged only by the effort to get inside the other to see what information is needed to have meaning made clear. This is a position an adult who appreciates the problem can take up to bridge the communication gap between the adult and the child.

If children are to be able to take part in dialogue, they must see others' needs for information; this is learning they can accomplish only through dialogue, and only with the help of adults who understand their difficulties. Adults can help children turn back to consider what they know that is relevant and make a selection to communicate to the others. Children's skills of communication are developed through talk with others in which they are helped alternatively to project into others' needs for information and to reflect on the relevant knowledge they hold.

In engaging children in experiences of this kind, adults must always be projecting into children's problems of meanings, trying to select questions and comments that will help children reflect on their own knowledge and draw out what is needed for the listener. Adults must indicate this need for information and help children recognize the problem the listeners have in grasping the children's meanings. In this way, children are gradually helped to establish skills in using language that make communication with others effective.

Moreover, as children learn skills of dialogue, they are being involved in the ways in which adults think. Dialogue provides children with a model for thinking which may serve them when adults are no longer there to help. Research gives support to this view (Bruner, 1975; Luria & Yudovich, 1959; Vygotsky, 1962). Marion Blank's practical application of this principle has shown that carefully structured dialogue can help children who have considerable problems communicating and learning (Blank & Solomon, 1968).

It seems likely that differences in children's skills of using language are the results of differences in talk with adults that children meet continually in their homes. The majority of children have experiences of talk at home which provide an adequate basis for developing vocabulary and a range of language structures but the differences in the purposes for which talk is used in the home produce very different expectations about the use of talk, different skills in using language, and different ways of viewing their experiences.

How then might children's experiences of talk at home be related to their success in learning to read? In her study of the preschool experiences of young fluent readers, Margaret Clark found that all had parents who were interested in their children as developing individuals, who enjoyed their children's responses and interest in the world around them, and who were involved in talking to their children about their experiences and helping them to understand (Clark, 1976). In our own study, no data were collected on reading achievement when the children were 5, but a reading test was given when the children were 7. At that time, all the children except one of parents with educational advantage had a reading age well above their chronological age. The reading age of the one exception was about level with her chronological age, and her parents considered that she needed help. She proved to have a specific perceptual disability which hindered both reading and spelling.

But for children of parents with educational disadvantages the picture was very different. Few of these children had reading ages above their chronological age; the majority clustered around a level commensurate with their chronological age. Several operated at a level considerably below their chronological age, and one boy had not yet begun to read. The parents did not feel this was anything they could help with and they did not press the school to take action. A difference of about 10 IQ points was also found in the mean IQ at this age but all were still of average or above average intelligence.

The possibility that there is a close association among children's experiences of using language, the skills they develop, and their achievement in reading needs further investigation. It is perhaps justifiable to infer that the way in which children use language is to some extent a reflection of the structure they have recognized or are imposing on the experience. Their talk is not only a reflection of their strategies for examining and interpreting their experiences but, in younger children at least, talk is a means through which they make themselves aware of their own operations and responses.

What might be inferred about the skills children can bring to bear on their experiences of learning to read, from the evidence of their skills in using language? What differences in the children's preparedness for reading might result from differences in children's use of language?

The findings of our longitudinal study lead us to consider the following as possibilities to be investigated:

Children who are oriented toward reporting on detail and sequence, and who use different ways of making comparisons, may have an underlying search orientation which leads them to distinguish significant patterns. An orientation to search for detail and make comparisons may lead to an awareness of the significance of small differences in letter forms and in patterns of letters in words. It may lead to an awareness of differences in sounds and in patterns of sounds. An orientation to search for sequence may lead to an awareness of the significance in the order of letters and an awareness that significant differences must be attached to differences in the sequencing of letters and words.

Children who are oriented toward reasoning may look for ways of making sense of any task and may be more likely to adopt problem solving approaches. In viewing print they may more readily make sense of the task, looking for overall meaning, and they may be more aware of incongruity in meaning and use it as a check as they decode.

Children who are disposed to anticipate and predict readily may look for meanings that "fit" in order to fill gaps in decoding and use anticipated meanings as a checking device. The orientation to project into the experiences of others may mean that children pick up clues from other readers because they try to take the other's stance. They may immediately gain meaning from what they read because they project into the meanings as they decode and this may provide the motivation to persist with learning to read.

Children who learn to imagine readily through their experience of using language may not only have inner resources for interpreting stories, and an interest and involvement that will carry them along in spite of difficulties, but it is possible that the route through which the concepts of symbols and signs have been built up means that interpretation is immediate and vivid. If, in addition, children are familiar with books and stories and place value on books, they may have a repertoire of skills and the orientation to apply them seems likely to give them a preparedness for reading that will guarantee immediate take off when reading begins.

There is much to be investigated here; but if there is a relationship between children's experiences of using language, the skills they develop and their preparedness for reading this, then, must lead us to examine the experiences we provide during the early years in school for those children who have not developed these most essential skills.

References

Ackerman, P.D. Final report for story repetition and early language development. Department of Psychology, Wichita State University, 1976.

Bakher-Renes, H., & Joefhaghe-Hohle, M. Situatie verschillen in toolgebruck. Master's thesis, University of Amsterdam, 1974.

Bennett, M. *Teaching styles and pupil progress.* London: Open Books, 1976.

Bernstein, B. *Class, codes, and control,* Vol. 1. London: Routledge and Kegan Paul, 1971.

Bruner, J.S. The ontogenesis of speech acts. *Journal of Child Language,* 1975, *2,* 1-19.

Clark, M.M. *Reading difficulties in school.* Harmondsworth: Penguin, 1970.

Clark, M.M. *Young fluent readers.* London: Heinemann, 1976.

Davie, R., Butler, N.R., & Goldstein, H. *From birth to seven.* London: Longman, 1972.

Department of Education and Science. *Children and their primary schools* (The Plowden report). HMSO, 1967.

Department of Education and Science. *A language for life* (The Bullock report). HMSO, 1975.

Department of Education and Science. *Primary education in England.* HMSO, 1978.

Donachy, W. Parent participation in preschool education. *British Journal of Educational Psychology,* 1976, *46,* 31-39.

Durkin, D. *Children who read early.* New York: Teachers College Press, 1966.

Galton, M., Simon, B., & Croll, P. *Inside the primary classroom.* London: Routledge and Kegan Paul, 1980.

Halliday, M.A.K. *Learning how to mean.* London: Arnold, 1975.

Hess, R.D., & Shipman, V. Early experience and the socialization of cognitive modes in children. *Child Development, 36,* 867-886.

Irwin, O.C. Infant speech: Effects of systematic reading of stories. *Journal of Speech and Hearing Disorders,* 1960, *3,* 187-190.

Lazar, I., & Darlington, R.B. *Lasting effects after preschool.* U.S. Department of Health, Education and Welfare, OHDS 79-30178, 1978.

Little, A., Mabey, C., & Russell, J. Class size, pupil characteristics and reading attainment. In V. Southgate (Ed.), *Literacy at all levels.* London: Ward Lock Educational, 1972.

Luria, A.R., & Yudovitch, F.L. *Speech and the development of mental processes in the child.* Harmondsworth: Penguin, 1971.

Mitner, E. A study of the relationships between reading readiness in grade one and patterns of parent-child interaction. *Child Development,* 1951, *22,* 95-112.

Morris, J. *Reading in the primary school.* London: Newnes, 1959.

Morris, J. *Standards and progress in reading.* Slough: NFER, 1966.

Sestini, E. Maternal values and modes of communication. Unpublished master of philosophy thesis, University of Louisiana, 1975.

Snow, C.E., et al. Mother's speech in three social classes. *Journal of Psycholinguistic Research,* 1976, *5,* 1-20.

Snow, C.E., & Ferguson, C.A. (Eds.). *Talking to children: Language input and acquisition.* Cambridge: Cambridge University Press, 1977.

Snow, C.E. Conversations with children. In P. Fletcher & M. Gorman (Eds.), *Studies in language acquisition*. Cambridge: Cambridge University Press, 1979.

Tough, J. *The development of meaning*. London: Allen and Unwin, 1977.

Wells, C.G. Variations in child language. In V. Lee (Ed.), *Language development*. London: Croom Helm, 1979.

Vygotsky, L. *Thought and language*. Cambridge, Massachusetts: MIT press, 1962.

Beginning Reading Development: Strategies and Principles

Yetta M. Goodman
University of Arizona

Many of my colleagues in the field of reading support a model of reading as a psycholinguistic guessing game. They say, "It's a model which seems to describe the developing reader well but certainly that's not how kids learn to read. A carefully controlled reading program is necessary at the beginning stages."

This statement was a challenge to me and since 1971 I have been on a search to find out more about the onset of learning to read. All of the work done in relation to the Goodman Model of Reading (1980) suggests that processing written language is similar to processing oral language so I looked to the research on oral language development to understand more about the development of written language.

In order to understand the beginnings of oral language development, linguists and psycholinguists studied 2, 3, and 4 year olds. They were amazed at what young children know about language at such an age. Though children cannot talk about this knowledge, their daily language use provides insight into it. Now psychologists are looking at children only a few months old to gain additional insights into the process of oral language development.

I began to wonder what we could discover about the emergence of reading and writing by studying very young children before, it is commonly assumed, beginning reading occurs. As my own work developed I became aware of an international group of scholars who were also beginning to think about young children and their interactions with print: Reid (1966), Clay (1975), Smith (1965), Downing (1970), Soderburgh (1977), Read (1975), and Ferreiro (1980). A number of questions emerged. In a print-oriented society, do children develop an intuitive awareness of the nature of print at 2, 3, and 4 years of age? Do most children, in some sense, learn to read prior to schooling? As researchers, have we overlooked this early learning of written language because our models have caused us to ignore what is happening in the child's head? Have we so confused literacy development with schooling that we have ignored what children learn about written language prior to formal instruction?

I began to study children from the ages of 2 through 6. I used print which I expected to be familiar to them from TV, streets, freeways, and supermarkets. I asked them to handle books and newspapers in various ways.

I am interested in written language development, not because I believe reading should be taught in kindergarten or preschools. Rather, if we can discover 1) how children learn to interact with print in the real world; 2) what developmental patterns are involved in written language acquisition; 3) what significant features of written language children attend to; and 4) the nature of written language development, then we can set up curricula which build on the knowledge about written language which children bring to school.

Based on the research and theories of these scholars, and my own research with preschoolers, I have some tentative conclusions. Many 2, 3, and 4 year old children are learning to read by themselves through their interactions with print. This self-teaching happens only in literate societies and cultures where print bombards the senses of children. Think of the streets and supermarkets where preschoolers walk, the highways young children are driven along, and the written displays they encounter on TV. Children learn to organize and make sense of print just as they learn to organize the rest of their world. As they understand how four-legged animals differ from two-legged animals, they learn that print says things in one way while pictures say things in another. Early in my own research, I realized that preschoolers would often point to print and ask, "What does that say?" They were aware that print communicates—that it involves an act of meaning. Reading begins at this point of awareness.

Beginning reading at this stage is not alphabetic. Children are aware that print does the telling but view the written display as symbols of meaning. Therefore, the cut-out front panel of Rice Krispies is cereal, the Crest panel is toothpaste, and Pepsi Cola can be called Pepsi, Coke, pop, or soda. Interestingly, children most often respond appropriately within the category of items. Even though they may know the names of some letters, understanding the alphabetic nature of written language comes later. The important questions for children seem to be, "What is written language for? What does it mean?" Through this exploration, children begin to make all kinds of intuitive decisions about *how* written language means. This supports Halliday's notion that form follows function (1975). Just like proficient readers do, young children use the print and its meaning, interacting with it through their own knowledge about the world—their own developing system of language and concepts. In addition they use pictorial cues, including color and situational context. Given a cut-out from a McDonald's French fries envelope, one child yelled, "That's McDonald's French fries!" She only had a two-dimensional form but could construct what the whole was from her previous experience. "Where does it say McDonald's French fries?" we asked, and the child pointed to the small black boldface letters, moving her fingers from left to right saying "McDonald's French fries" quickly and moving her finger slowly so it all came out even. She could have pointed to a whole line of golden arches, but rejected that graphic display as the written language communicator. This child is using the whole situation to construct meaning but knows it's the print that does the telling or saying of the meaning. One more example can support this point. We use a magazine picture of a large automobile in our studies. As the picture comes in view, our subjects most often say "car." "Where does it say car?" we ask.

Goodman

Our subjects will respond by quickly finding a very small printed Chevrolet in the upper left-hand corner and moving their fingers back and forth under the printed word.

When print is totally decontextualized, preschoolers no longer treat it as meaningful language. For example, given a wrapper (pasted on a cardboard) which says Ivory in large blue letters on a design of blue and white wavy lines, there is enough context so that almost all of our 3 and 4 year olds respond with either "soap" or "Ivory." When the word Ivory is printed in manuscript on plain white paper, the little ones react in three different ways. Some respond immediately with, "You know I can't read." Others start naming the letters, often, but not always, appropriately. One 4 year old who read Ivory and pointed to the appropriate print in the earlier contextualized task, pointed to each letter saying, "One-five-zero-r-e." The third group acted bored, fidgety, or silly. Being able to read in a situationally embedded context but not out of it is similar to the way young children develop oral language.

Bloom (1970) says children talk about events that are immediately perceptually available in the nonlinguistic context— adults do not talk about what they see and what they are doing when a listener is there to see for himself. It appears that child utterances depend directly on the support of nonlinguistic context, whereas adult utterances do not. This seems to be as true of written language development as it is of oral.

Use of Reading Strategies

Children make use of all the reading strategies described by the Goodman Model of the reading process (1980). Early on, readers recognize print and select the cues they believe to be significant. One 4 year old subject, upon seeing a label from Chicken of the Sea tuna, said, "That's chicken, no, tuna!" She then concluded, "No, dog food." Her first prediction was based on some cue from the graphic print *chicken*; she then realized it was not really chicken by picking up additional cues. We're not sure which ones, but she disconfirmed her original prediction as she changed her response to *tuna*. We couldn't understand the "dog food" response until one the research assistants noticed a red and white checkered symbol on the can which is the symbol used by the Ralston Purina Company, the manufacturer of dog food which also manufactures Chicken of the Sea tuna. With a lot of experience with a variety of print in many different situations, readers learn which are the significant language cues and which are not. It is very important to be selective in language learning and language use. Our early readers show they are beginning to be selective. They'll need lots of experience with real print in natural language environments to set it all straight.

Another predicting example comes from a 4 year old who responded to the picture of a Chevrolet by saying, "Bruick." "Where does it say Bruick?" I asked. He pointed to the small print in the upper part of the picture (Chevrolet) and said, "No, it's a Cadillac; no that's a Chevette. I thought it was a Bruick 'cause my auntie drives one."

Confirmation strategies are shown in both of the previous examples. In each case, the subjects use their knowledge to select minimum cues and predict. They disconfirm their initial guesses and responses and select additional cues to come up with responses more satisfactory to themselves. Through these examples it is obvious that young readers are using print embedded in a known context to construct meaning.

Young readers are also tentative. They begin to form generalizations about the alphabetic nature of print and often begin to know when they do not know. Three year olds are quick to respond to Rice Krispies as cereal, while 5 year olds may respond more slowly. They may respond initially with, "I don't know," but when encouraged to guess, some say, "It's not Raisin Bran." or "I know it's some kind of cereal." I believe these children are at a more mature stage than the quick-to-respond 3 year olds. By 5, children begin to relate sounds to letters and to know that names should be specific, not generic. With their greater knowledge, they become more tentative, acting as if they know less than some of the 3 year olds.

As children develop concepts about print, the labels they use may be inappropriate. Although in responding to print in context, 3 year olds often respond with a two word response for a two word text item; they will use the terms *word, letter,* and *number* interchangeably. It is important to realize that these terms are all conceptually related. In addition, children can use language appropriately in context but when asked to define the same item, they often cannot. For example, part of the task we have given our readers is book handling. I hold up a page in a book, wave it back and forth and say, "What is this?" None of the twelve 3 and 4 year olds I last did this with could answer the question. However, as I read them a story and came to the end of the print on the page, I'd say, "What should I do now?" Everyone of the children I asked replied, "Turn the *page.*" Using language appropriately in a common, real experience setting is much easier than defining a term or explaining what something is in the abstract.

Principles of Beginning Reading Development

So far I have provided a general picture of what children do in response to print and some tentative conclusions about written language development. As children interact with print, they not only begin to read and write—that is, actually use reading and writing for various purposes—they begin to develop principles about the nature and meaning of written language. They begin to decide what aspects of written language are significant for communication to take place and which aspects are insignificant and merit little attention. Designers of commercial logos make use of color. Color seems to be a feature of familiar print which provides some cue to aid in prediction early in development, but children soon seem to respond almost as well to the same print environment when color is missing. For example, children respond to a black and white reproduction of a stop sign, McDonald's, or Ivory almost the same as to the item retaining the original color.

Children construct a variety of principles about language relevant to their developing literacy, though they may essentially need to discard some and construct others if they are to move on. For a period of time, some of these principles may actually interfere with the development of other principles which may be more important. For example, if a child decides that in order for an aspect of language to be readable it must have no less than three characters or letters (Ferreiro, 1980) then at some point a conflict or disequilibrium develops between concepts of wordness related to a minimal number principle and the reality of words such as *in, on*, or phrases such as *he is to go to a Dr.* To complicate matters even further, many of these developing principles overlap and interact and children have to sort out which principles are most significant to meaning in written language and which are not very useful, are used infrequently, or have no relationship to reading or writing. Most important for everyone involved in curriculum development, however, is that these principles really cannot be taught through traditional, structured reading programs. Rather, they develop as children personally interact with a great deal of written language in appropriate environmental contexts which highlight the need for written language and the significant functions it serves.

These principles, I believe, emerge idiosyncratically for each child. Some principles may be considered together from the beginning and others may not. Children may reject one principle for another, depending on the text, the item, the significance of the reading or writing experience to the child, or the function of any particular literacy event. Also, children may decide that certain principles have certain qualities in reading but are different for writing and still different for spelling or for talking about writing. For example, when Denise wrote her name, she wrote each letter with a capital letter except for the *i* which was the same size as the others except dotted: DENiSE. As she formed each letter, she said, "dee...eee...em...ell...see...eee." After she was finished, she was asked, "Now tell me, what does that say?" She responded, "Denise Roberts." When asked, "Can you read that?" she looked at each letter as she responded appropriately, "D...E...N...I...S...E." Reading, saying, and spelling as one writes do not all result in the same kinds of productions. Different principles seem to be operating in each one of these situations.

Goodman

In my research on the roots of literacy (1980) and through an awareness of the research of others, I have begun to delineate these principles as I understand them at the present time. Additional research will cause adaptations, changes, or deletions in the principles and their various aspects; other principles will be expanded and developed. The more researchers gain insight into which principles children develop, how they are used and how they develop, the more we'll understand about written language development.

What's most significant, in my case, is that children are involved in developing a writing system for themselves. In many ways, as individuals, they are going through the same problems and raising the same questions for themselves that the world's communities went through when they became literate. The needs, the environment, the attitudes, the knowledge, the significant others are all merging to aid each child in becoming a literate human being. If the significance of each "literary event" (any experience with reading and writing in which the child is involved) in the life of the child is not well understood, educators will continue for hundreds of years to teach children aspects of linguistic study which they do not need prior to the development of literacy and will ignore the intuitive knowledge children have when they come to school. This intuitive knowledge about the principles of written language is their greatest asset in becoming literate.

The major principles are best viewed as developmental, since children grow into and through all of them. They develop idiosyncratically, depending on each child's environment, and they overlap and become integrated. Over time, children must sort out which principles are the most significant in any particular written language event or situation. The three major kinds of principles include: 1) functional principles which emerge as children discover when and how written language is used and for what purposes; 2) linguistic principles which emerge as children discover how written language is organized in relation to the graphophonic syntactic, semantic, and pragmatic systems of language; and 3) relational principles which emerge as children discover how the systems, units, or aspects of written and/or oral languages relate to the systems, units, or aspects of meaning or how they relate to each other.

Functional Principles

Functional principles develop through children's responses to specific uses of literacy. The degree to which literacy events are meaningful and the value that any particular literacy event has for any particular child in any particular cultural setting will have impact on the development of the functional principles. Most written language which the child experiences can be divided into two categories: 1) print in environmental settings (on TV; names for people, toys, games; print used to direct and control our lives on streets and highways and in buildings and stores) and 2) print embedded in connected discourse, which includes more traditional forms of written language (books, magazines, comics, newspapers, letters). Experiences with print will be different for different children. Children whose parents are college students, computer programers, or authors, where a great deal of writing and reading goes on in the home, will discover the significance of literacy events differently from children whose parents may read only the Bible daily before dinner or children whose parents use writing selectively for shopping lists, filling out forms, and taking phone messages. The statements adults and siblings make about literacy events also have their effect on children's developing notions about the function of literacy. Negative statements about schooling, the ability to read and write, and the difficulty of reading and writing will have as much impact on children's developing literacy as the influence of enjoyment in books and reading. Literate parents who show anxiety about literacy development in young children and denigrate the schooling experience may leave marks on the child's view of the value of reading and writing and its learning in the school setting. Educators can do little about these situations in any immediate sense. It is important, though, to build awareness of the impact of home experiences on literacy development through parent and community education. We know children are influenced differently by the great diversity of literacy events in developing ideas and concepts about the function of written language in the society by the time they come to school (Wells, 1980). Significantly, however, children encountering literacy events will construct important knowledge about the nature and function of print in their daily lives many years prior to schooling. Children will show through their responses that some functions of written language in the environment control the lives of others. Jon, as he passed a school sign, said to his mother, "That says 'watch out for kids.'" Darryl's mom was driving him to school and stopped by a Park Parallel sign to let him out near the school playground. He pointed at the sign and said to his mom, "Ya better not park here." Roberta may have been indicating that the names of people and the names of places serve similar functions when she said to her mother as they were driving past the drug chain, "Revco had the same face as my name." By age 4, some children know that newspapers serve many functions. A number of 4 year olds, shown the advertising page in the newspaper, responded with: "Take that to the market," "Buy ketchup," or "It says coffee costed less." When shown the TV page, they said: "Channel four," "Sesame Street," or another favorite program. These children are categorizing and organizing the function of one form of written language in their world. They even discover their own personal use for written language. Reis was scolded one day for leaving the house and not letting his mother know where he went. The next day, when his mother was looking for him, she found this note on the table. It said, "IMGOEGTOOBAWTSID." (I'm going to be outside.) When you don't have an immediate face-to-face situation, written language, this child discovered, can be used for long distance communication.

A 7 year old was very concerned about a problem she had. Instead of confronting her mother directly, she decided that if she wrote a note it might soften matters somewhat. Her mother found the following on her pillow when she woke up in the morning:

Dear Mom   plese don't get mad
I dremed that i was sitting on
the toylit
you no what I mean do you and by axidint
i pede my bed

When children write shopping lists or lists for Santa Claus, they most often place one item appropriately after the previous one. Not only have they learned the function of lists, but they seem to know something about the form as well. Children discover a variety of functions of written language through everyday literacy events, but through story reading they learn the function of connected discourse. They are able to point to the print in books when someone asks, "Can you show me where I am reading?" Children who are not as personally involved in book reading may point to the picture as the place adults are reading. Also a child will show the function of language in books through reading a book even without words by starting on an appropriate beginning page and saying in an appropriate tone, "Once upon a time." Children discover the function of written language through every literacy event in their experience. If those events are positive, warm, and significant to their lives, children will grow into literacy easily and naturally. Literacy events may be unpleasant or meaningless for some children; for them, growth into literacy will seem to be an overwhelming chore.

Linguistic Principles

A second group of principles is linguistic in nature. The child comes to know: 1) how the written language system is organized, 2) what its units are, 3) which features are most significant, and 4) the stability of its organization.

For example, children learning English develop notions about the alphabetic nature of the written language while Chinese children develop notions about the logographic nature of writing. English language children must come to know that the alphabet includes letters such as B K A, and not such letters as רׁ פֿכ as in Hebrew. Many children play at making letters or characters before they know that letters have names or that letters are related to reading and writing. English children's letters look remarkably like the alphabetic system known as English, while Arabic children's letters have the sweep and character of the Arabic alphabet. Over time, children discover that English words have a specific pattern or organization and this is revealed through their invented spellings. They become aware, especially as they read and write stories, that punctuation is used for a variety of purposes. They sometimes begin using punctuation before they have total control over its function and purposes. Other times they experiment with punctuation in nonconventional ways. Rudy, age 6, used periods instead of spaces to show word boundaries for a time in his development of the writing system.

As children learn that written language takes up space, directionality of the written language system and the various forms it takes are also developed. Although in schools we are sometimes concerned that children write from right to left, we take it for granted that almost all of these children do write horizontally and not vertically. In most cases, when children are asked to show where it says something, they move their fingers from left to right and sometimes from right to left across the print. Early in their schooling, they seem to know that the story in a book goes from the top line to the bottom and across to the next page.

Observation of children as they write often shows their developing control over directionality. They may start their explorations into directionality by writing in the same way they draw. It goes in many directions and it doesn't make any difference where it starts or ends. Soon more deliberate directionality is observable.

When Bryan was 3½, he drew a large dinosaur on the right side of a large sheet of paper. When he finished his drawing, he was at the bottom of the paper but he wanted to write the name of the dinosaur so he asked for the spelling and as he was given the letters, he wrote *ty* on the bottommost part of the paper and ran *usor us rex* each on separate lines because of the amount of space left snaking up to the top of the page. He was writing from left to right and returning to the beginning of the line each time, but the direction he went seemed to relate to the spacing of his drawing and aesthetic qualities rather than all the appropriate writing conventions. Since we have not observed children carefully in their writing development during these periods of time, we have been ignorant of the development toward horizontal directionality by English children. We become nervous when we look at a finished piece of writing, see it in reverse order, and assume that something is organically wrong with the writer. Most children, except the hearing impaired and some other nonvocal handicapped youngsters, generally control the linguistic principles of oral language prior to the development of written language. Many of the syntactic and semantic aspects of oral language are similar to written language. However, directionality, space, and form in written language have no counterpart in oral language and children need to organize this system from the beginning as they use it. They also must develop ideas about spelling; punctuation; and variations in spacing, topography, and handwriting, as well as aesthetic uses of written language. None of the these features are obvious in oral language, so children need to explore written language and its components widely in order to understand the complexities of writing as a system. This is developed through use. Children most easily control those aspects of the syntactic and semantic systems which are similar in both oral and written language. However, some features of written language occur only in that system. Direct quotes are used frequently in children's literature and are not often part of oral language. Children represent direct quotes in their own writing very early without conventional space and punctuation until later in their development.

Relational Principles

Children learn to relate written language to meaning and where necessary to oral language. They develop the knowledge that some unit of written language is linked in some way with some unit of meaning or some unit of oral, or both. This linkage may be words or letters but it is not restricted to them. It also includes propositions, ideas, concepts, images, signs, symbols, and icons.

Early in their development, children may develop the belief that somehow written language should express in writing some of the characteristics of the object being described. Therefore, it is not surprising that Ferreiro (1980), in using

Piagetian type tasks in written language, concludes that children often use the size of the object, the characteristics or the number of items being referred to, or their age. "Father's name must have more letters than mine because he is so much bigger and older than I am." Or, if *kitten* is written with three characters, then *three kittens* is written by reduplicating the same set of characters three times. Again, the active development of children's involvement in their own written language development is evident. As children develop the notion that written language is alphabetic, both the phonological system and the graphic system of language becomes interrelated. The child may write AED at the end of a story. Usually at this stage, the child is generalizing the sound that *e* represents in words such as bent, and set to the letter *A*. (Read, 1975, explains this sophisticated decision in his study of children's phonological development.) When asked why there is both an *A* and an *E* in that word (AED), one child said, "It has to have three and that letter has to be *D* 'cause it's at the end. It's got an *E* in it, but I know it has to have an *A* here." The child cannot fully articulate the complicated graphophonic relationships taking place, but a careful analysis of this and other aspects of children's spelling suggests a complicated interrelationship developing between the graphic and sound systems of language.

It is not uncommon to find children using a *Y* or an *E* at the end of words to represent the silent *E* or *Y*. *Play* and *make* have been spelled as *plae* and *maky*. Think of the complex relationships and rules children must work through: *Y* often represents the sound of *E* in final positions in many dialects of American English as in *kitty, Betty, marry*. In addition, both *Y* and *E* are final markers and each can be in final positions without having its own sound representation but patterning with other letters in order to represent sounds. Both *make* and *play* are good examples of this latter phenomenon. As in so many other areas of language, children's errors or miscues provide considerable insight into their developing knowledge of the principles of written language.

During their development children also relate story structure and voice pointing to written language. They indicate as they start to "read" a book that they know it has a story structure. They use phrases such as *"Mother said," "The witch cried,"* as they repeat a book they've heard read to them often. They will start such a book with a story opener such as "Once upon a time" or "A long, long time ago." These are all aspects of language which tend to occur in written texts for children. As they use these written language forms, they show they know that certain kinds of language occur in certain texts and not in others. Given a joke or riddle book, children change the kinds of language they use. They relate certain kinds of language to certain kinds of written texts. They have insights into the context of the situation.

Another kind of relational principle develops as children seem to discover that the written line and the oral utterance have some relationship in common in certain contexts. After Ramon has responded to Kellogg's Raisin Bran with, "That's cereal," he was asked, "Can you show me where it says cereal?" He swept his finger under the main print, Kellogg's Raisin Bran, and said slowly, "Cee...ree...aal," so that his voice and finger pointing ended at the same point. Eventually, as children are read to or asked to follow along as an adult reads, there is evidence that they are developing ways of relating the oral and written language. Clay (1980) has called this phenomenon "voice pointing."

Children need active experiences with literacy in order to grow and develop the roots of literacy (Goodman, 1980). Through such active experiences with literacy events, children develop principles about written language. We can't teach these principles. Children construct them through interactions with their literate environment and through asking questions about it. What we can do as teachers is to organize a literate environment that will invite children to interact and to ask questions.

References

Bloom, L. *Language development: Form and function in emerging grammars.* Cambridge, Massachusetts: MIT Press, 1970.

Clay, M. *What did I write?* Auckland: Heineman Educational Books, 1975.

Clay, M. *Patterns of complex behavior.* Auckland: Heineman Educational Books, 1980.

Downing, J. Children's concepts of language in learning to read. *Educational Research*, 1970.

Ferreiro, E. *Los sistemas de escritura en el desarrollo del niño* (with A. Teberosky). Mexico: Siglo, 21 Ed., 1979.

Ferreiro, E. The relationship between oral and written language: The children's view-points. Presentation at Impact of Child Language Development Research on Curriculum and Development, 1980.

Goodman, K.S. *Reading of American children whose reading is a stable, rural dialect of English or language other than English.* Grant No. NIE-C-00-3-0087. National Institute of Education, U.S. Department of Health, Education and Welfare, 1978.

Goodman, Y. Roots of literacy. In M.P. Douglass (Ed.), *Claremont reading conference forty-fourth yearbook.* Claremont, California: 1980, 1-32.

Halliday, M.A.K. *Learning how to mean: Explorations in the development of language.* New York: Elsevier, 1975.

Read, C. *Children's categorization of speech sounds in English.* NCTE Research Report # 17. Urbana, Illinois: National Council of Teachers of English, 1975.

Reid, J.F. Learning to think about reading. *Educational Research,* 1966, *9,* 56-62.

Smith, F. Learning to read by reading. *Language Arts,* 1976, 297-299.

Soderburgh, R. *Reading in early childhood: A linguistic study of a preschool child's gradual acquisition of reading ability.* Washington, D.C.: Georgetown University Press, 1977.

Wells, G. *Learning through interaction: The study of language development.* Cambridge University Press, 1981.

Part Three
Writing and Reading: What For?

Birnbaum and Emig bring the constructivist perspective to this illuminating examination of the processes of reading and writing. Both processes, they argue, involve the active construction of meaning: one, writing through text and the other, reading from text. In this respect, both consist of complex, continuous, increasingly coordinated acts of mind. Moreover, the processes appear to be mutually interacting and, thus, mutually influential in development.

At the same time, the processes are also markedly different. Readers and writers stand in different relations to texts: one creates the text, the other re-creates it. The reader makes meaning through anticipating the unfolding of a given text; the other interacts with her own evolving text, anticipating where it will go and taking clues from where it has come.

Both reading and writing share common developmental origins, though here the view is presented that writing develops earlier. In literate cultures, both processes develop naturally, from everyday experience of print, as Goodman (this volume) also argues. Unfortunately, this naturally developing literacy is short-circuited by school practices, especially for writing.

With this unique view of the similarities and differences of the two processes in mind, both developmentally and functionally, Nancy Martin and Louise Rosenblatt offer us speculations on the purposes of these two processes in the lives of people. They ask what writing and reading are for and what role they might best play in adult life.

Martin notes that what we conceive writing to be, and to be for, arises from our experience of writing—especially our school experience. Two aspects of our school experience of writing are crucial in the value we assign to writing as adults. These aspects she calls models and contexts. Models are the examples of writing, repeatedly encountered, from which we construct our views of its use and form. For young children, the most useful models are those which have something in common with their language and viewpoint—usually stories, poems, plays, and forms of "personal language." From their encounters with these models, children construct a sense of what they can do with written language.

Unfortunately, children encounter few models of good transactional writing. Thus, at the end of childhood, when society legislates against personal or poetic writing, children have no useful models of informational or persuasive writing to draw on, particularly not any to which they can commit themselves.

Contexts, Martin asserts, include the attitudes and beliefs of teachers, which directly affect the social and intellectual climate of schools. Drawing on her investigations of school contexts in Western Australian secondary schools, she notes that teacher support of students' intentions for writing, and commitment to relationships and to learning, were the features of the context most directly influencing the quality of students' writing.

Reading, as Rosenblatt argues, involves a transaction between whole persons and texts. Readers can undertake this transaction, through which meaning is constructed, in two distinct ways: efferently or aesthetically. In the former, the concern is with "building public meaning that is to be carried away from the reading"; in the latter, the concern is with "what is being lived through *during* the reading." Readers can choose which stance to take in each situation of reading and, therefore, choose what sort of transaction to have with the text.

Mature readers are those persons who can adopt appropriate stances: appropriate to their individual powers and purposes, to the situation of reading, and to the text. Education can help readers to develop competence in the use of both stances and to learn when to use which one. To do this, Rosenblatt notes, schools will have to eradicate the current efferent bias and to give fuller, more informed, and more balanced attention to the aesthetic—and all that implies for readers, as persons, and for their lifelong transactions with texts.

Creating Minds, Created Texts: Writing and Reading

June Birnbaum
Janet Emig
Rutgers University

Writing and reading: What are the immensely complex relations between the two processes of verbal literacy conceptually? Developmentally? Pedagogically? Politically?

Conceptualizations of Writing and Reading

Both ultimate positions can be swiftly dismissed: 1) that the processes bear no relation to one another and 2) that the two processes are identical. Both are so absurd that readers may wonder if we have not created them. There are, however, powerful proponents for both views. Those who hold the first view tend to not state it abstractly but to reveal it through curricular decisions and actions. Two examples, one from an elementary school and the other from a university. Currently, in many American elementary schools, from 45 to 120 minutes a day are devoted exclusively to reading and to what administrators and teachers regard as such concomitant skills as word attack and comprehension skills and vocabulary building. Of that time, Smith (1982) estimates that as few as four minutes may be allotted children for whole reading experiences. If writing instruction appears at all in these schools, it is separated in time and place from reading instruction and in contexts where no parallels can readily be drawn between the processes. For example, children know that they write stories, but they do not know that the texts they read have authors. Moreover, much that passes for writing instruction is actually drill in usage, punctuation, and mechanics, divorced from production of whole texts.

Wholly discrete undergraduate or graduate programs in reading and in writing at colleges and universities are also statements that the two processes bear so little relation that they do not require being considered together. Departments of English that treat student writing only in isolated special programs are really departments of literature, just as language arts curricula in many elementary schools are actually reading programs exclusively.

Researchers rather than classroom teachers seem to espouse the second ultimate position. Shanahan (1980), describing much of the current psycholinguistic-based research, notes that without a program note a reviewer cannot "readily distinguish between characterizations of reading and of writing" (p. 360). Yet the two processes are clearly separable and distinct. Consider the following two statements: 1) "I read *Pride and Prejudice*" and 2) "I wrote *Pride and Prejudice*." Almost all of us can make the first claim; none of us can make the second—a situation logically impossible if the two propositions contained identical content.

Other views of the relation between writing and reading— less ultimate, if no less misguided—appear in the literature. There is, for example, the pervasive view that the processes are the inverse of one another: a reader follows the same linguistic-cognitive steps in inverse order as the writer followed in creating the text. A common metaphor representing this conceptualization is the mirror image. Ruddell (1969), Page (1974), and de Beaugrande (1979) have implicitly deployed the mirror metaphor in their descriptions of the reading and writing processes.

According to de Beaugrande, for example, the writer follows eight stages that may occur sequentially and recursively. The writer
1. evolves an intention for writing;
2. decides upon a plan for achieving the intention;

3. chooses a mode of discourse;
4. selects a topic or set of topics out of the general domain of experience;
5. selects aspects of the topic to be emphasized;
6. assigns associated properties to those aspects and arranges these into a basic structure of meaning;
7. assigns actual language to these aspects; and
8. arranges the language in a linear sequence according to syntactic and rhetorical choices.

Then, if the text motivates, the reader will reverse the process described in steps 6, 7, and 8 to recover the basic structure of the writer's meaning and to gain new knowledge of the topic represented by the text.

There are curious assumptions embedded in the mirror model, at least as set out by de Beaugrande. W.H. Auden once said that he could distinguish a writer from a nonwriter by the response to his question "Where do you begin?" The nonwriter said with an idea; the writer gave him a word or phrase. In the de Beaugrande model, in contrast, thought and language remain separate for 7/8ths of the composing process, with language clothing the thought only near the culmination of the process. The verb de Beaugrande uses also reveals his curious view about the value and inevitability of language: the writer "*assigns* actual language" (italics ours) to meaning. The most or least that can be said about this view is that it demonstrates what Brown (1959) calls the cloak theory of the relation of thought and language: that language is merely a cloak that, arbitrarily and casually, is laid over the contours, the body of thought.

Regarding the text as a code that one *en*codes (writes) and then *de*codes (reads) shares assumptions with the mirror metaphor that the processes are again regarded linguistically and cognitively as the inverse of each other. What Read (1977), like Chomsky (1971), is finding in his research about young children presents compelling developmental evidence against the inverse point of view. In his article entitled "Why Writing Is Not the Inverse of Reading, for Young Children," Read notes that preschool and primary grade children frequently go through a stage in which reading and writing are not parallel: a stage in which they can read standard orthography fairly fluently, but in which they continue to write in their own nonstandard orthography, often called invented spelling. On the other hand, they write standard orthography or read their own invented spellings only with difficulty. In other words, they cannot read what they have just written. This imbalance suggests that reading and writing need not mirror each other in stages of development.

Many other theorists and practitioners express very strong doubt that so neat a reversal obtains. K. Goodman (1968) suggests that, although the two processes share a common cognitive-linguistic base, the role of surface features is different for the two. The writer of the text has no alternative but to attend closely to rules and conventions of syntax and rhetoric, even of spelling, to set forth a meaning. The reader, however may merely sample the surface text in his effort to ascertain the writer's meaning as embodied in the text, particularly if his major purpose is to carry information away from the text.

If the mirror image metaphor fails to explain the relationship, perhaps converging shifts in views of the two processes will suggest points where they intersect. In his 1977 review of the research concerning the role of schemata in reading behaviors, Anderson concluded that research in the field had moved from a bottom up view of reading as a passive word-by-word processing of text to a top down or interactionist view, with reading an active construction of the text emanating from the knowledge, purpose, and interest of the reader. (Huey, who had anticipated so much else of current work into writing as well as reading, espoused this definition of reading as a process as early as 1908.) Concurrently, research into the composing process underscored the disparity between the bottom up view of writing inherent in current teaching approaches and in textbooks such as Warriner's and actual writing behaviors (Emig, 1969; Graves, 1973; Perl, 1979; Pianko, 1977). Like reading, writing behaviors are dependent upon the knowledge, purpose, and interest of the writer. As the field shifted from a bottom up to a top down view of writing, there was increased interest in the writer's schemata for text production (Applebee, 1977; Bereiter, 1979; Brown,

1977; Flower, 1979) concomitant with research concerning the reader's schemata for text construction. This convergence in views suggests how the two processes may be related.

To make statements about the relationships between writing and reading is inevitably to commit those making the statements to a given theoretical position. We are no exception. What follows is a setting forth of a constructivist view concerning language and cognition as well as reading and writing. To espouse this point of view today is not to isolate ourselves conceptually but, rather, to place us in the majority community, a community with such members as Anderson (1977), Britton (1970), K. and Y. Goodman (1978), Graves (1978), F. Smith (1973, 1982), and Young, Becker, and Pike (1970).

Both processes represent the symbolic transformation of experience as Langer described in *Feeling and Form* (1953) and *Philosophy in a New Key* (1956): "The brain. . .following its own law. . .is actively translating experience into symbols, in fulfillment of a basic need to do so" (pp. 41-42). Eisner (1981) suggests that, in writing, vision is transformed into words; in reading, words into vision—both representing symbolic transformations.

Both processes are centrally concerned with the construction of meaning through text, a major mode of symbolic transformation. As Nystrand (1979) puts it: "The text should be the result of and the occasion for the constructive processes of the mind" (p. 238). Constructing meaning, then, is an active process of cognition.

Both are acts of skill in the sense Michael Polanyi describes in that they are "continuous, coordinated performances." We are not calling reading here wording aloud or making small lineal analyses of excerpted passages; and we are not calling writing disembodied and asyntactic responses either to actual events or to texts. Rather, we are describing both as acts of skill in Polanyi's phrase: "of doing more things at once than one can possibly think of."

Both skilled readers and writers seem able to employ behaviors in each process that span a spectrum of responses ranging from the extensive to the reflexive in writing (Emig,

1969) and from the efferent to the aesthetic in reading (Rosenblatt, 1938/1968, 1978). Recent findings indicate that individuals, whether reading or writing, tend to respond in parallel ways along each of these spectrums provided mode, subject, purpose, and setting are similar (Birnbaum, 1981).

Both reading and writing then as such acts of skill are processes of immense perceptual, experiential, linguistic, and cognitive complexity and, as such, fragile and vulnerable to interference and trauma. As Gardner (1975) notes in *The Shattered Mind: The Person after Brain Damage*, the abilities to read and to write are almost always impaired by any brain trauma, no matter the specific hemispheric site for that trauma.

The processes are mutually enhancing. Stotsky, in her broad 1975 review concerning how children's syntactic knowledge and sentence-combining activities affect writing abilities and reading comprehension, concludes that

> a significant crossover modal effect can theoretically occur, on the one hand, permitting speaking, listening, and reading activities to influence writing ability, and on the other hand permitting writing activities to enhance reading comprehension (p. 66).

Stotsky qualifies her conclusion about the impact of reading upon writing by emphasizing the importance of ability to reflect over language and suggesting that elementary grade students may be less able to deliberate over it than secondary students. Smith (1982) also hypothesizes that reading experiences enhance writing when students reflect over language with a writer's eye and develop a sensitivity that directs their attention to it. To date, most empirical studies of the reciprocal influences of reading and writing have been fragmentary and correlational.

These studies of such crossovers can be divided into two categories. In the first, investigators have compared subjects' performance on a single measure of reading achievement with level of syntactic maturity in writing derived from normed indices for the subjects' age levels (Evans, 1972; W. Smith, 1970); from tests of syntactic knowledge (Kuntz, 1975; Takahashi, 1975); or from syntactic complexity found in the subjects' own writing (Evanecko, Ollila, & Armstrong, 1974; Evans, 1979; Lazdowski,

1976). All reported finding a relationship between reading and writing levels, although both Takahashi and Evans reported some anomalies for part of their sample that led them to question the validity of their standardized reading tests as measures of syntactic comprehension.

A second group of investigators has attempted to promote achievement in one process through treatment of the other. Methods of intervention have included attempting to increase vocabulary used when writing 1) by teaching vocabulary found in the subjects' reading assignments (Wolfe, 1975); 2) by teaching sentence-combining skills in an effort to raise reading achievement scores (Crews, 1971; Hughes, 1975; Obenchain, 1972); and 3) by including a daily expressive writing component in a developmental reading course to improve reading achievement, self-esteem, and attitudes toward the two processes (Collins, 1979). Although Collins, Obenchain, and Wolfe reported gains for their secondary or college age experimental groups, Crews reported no gain for her fourth grade subjects. Hughes reported no gains for seventh grade subjects on a short standardized reading test, but gains by her experimental group in use of semantic and syntactic cueing systems on an oral reading sample. These findings may suggest that younger students with less mature cognitive development may be unable to reflect over experiences in one process sufficiently to influence ability in the other.

Undoubtedly, the most compelling evidence to date for a relationship between reading and writing comes from Loban's 13 year study of children's development (1976). His finding that children who were high achievers in one process tended to be high achievers in the other and that the oral language of older high achievers in reading and writing was marked by the use of hypothesis and conditionality suggests that proficiency in all language processes is rooted in shared cognitive and linguistic knowledge. Loban did not directly observe reading or writing behaviors but gathered his data from oral interviews with the students, samples of their writing, achievement test scores, and teacher ratings. Nevertheless, the length of the data gathering period makes his findings more persuasive than the single sample correlational studies.

Although the two processes share common cognitive and linguistic roots and seem capable of nurturing each other, apparent differences in their development must be recognized. The processes are markedly different as well. The nature of the text differs as the relation of writer and reader of the text differs. For the reader, a text in the sense of a graphic content, of words present on a page, exists "out there" as visible language. For the writer in the process of writing, the text is evolving or, in Pringle and Freedman's metaphor, unfolding (1979). The writer is originating the text: it had no existence before the writer gives it form-and-meaning. The writer is creating an object, an artifact, a not-I, palpable, existing in the world as a self-sustaining entity and event.

Rosenblatt has elegantly argued in this volume and elsewhere (1978) that the process of reading is the process of creating a poem from a text, with poem defined as each reader's unique response to the text. The writer initiates a text; a reader initiates a poem. In that sense, both are acts of creation. But the poem differs from the text in that it enjoys no independent life of its own; there can be no poem in her sense without a text that inspires it. The text is autonomous; the poem, dependent.

Making a text then (writing) as a process stays uniquely the act of autonomous initiation. In contrast, making a poem can be regarded as re-creative, as Dewey used that term in *Art as Experience* and Iser used it in *The Implied Reader*:

> For to perceive, the beholder must create his own experience. And his creation must include relations comparable to those the original producer underwent. They are not the same in any literal sense. But with the perceiver, as with the artist, there must be an ordering of the elements of the whole that is in form, although not in details, the same as the process of organization the creator of the work consciously experienced. Without an act of recreation the object is not perceived as a work of art. (1934/1958 p. 54)

Iser characterizes the act of reading as recreation:

> The act of recreation is not a smooth or continuous process, but one which, in its essence, relies on interruptions of the flow to render it

efficacious. We look forward, we look back, we decide, we change our decisions, we form expectations, we are shocked by their nonfulfillment, we question, we muse, we accept, we reject: this is the dynamic process of recreation. (1975 p. 288)

In a *Theory of Personality*, Kelly (1955) suggests that our central unique human activity is anticipation of events. Following Kelly, Frank Smith, like Goodman and many other reading theorists, suggests that the overarching process in reading is anticipating what the writer or the text will do: that skilled readers are skilled anticipators and predictors who can predict both globally and focally. Globally, they predict the nature and direction of the whole piece of discourse; focally, they predict the immediate—what segment of words-and-meaning to expect next.

Obviously, prediction by a reader of a text differs from predictions by its writer. In reading, a reader predicts what another has already done (if he was the writer, in rereading his own text, he changes his role to reader); in writing, the writer must predict and then enact what he will do next. Agent and tense of prediction for the two processes then differs as well, as does the requirement for the writer to provide the text.

Iser notes that in reading "we form expectations, we are shocked by their nonfulfillment." The role of surprise, logically, will differ for the processes of reading and of writing. The question may be "Do we accept more surprises from ourselves than from others?" Obviously, in writing and reading texts we can characterize as formulaic or algorithmic, we commit fewer surprises as writer and receive fewer surprises as reader. The valid use of the cloze technique is obviously predicated upon predicting exclusively from unsurprising, formulaic texts: it would have no validity at all if the text were *Finnegan's Wake* or *Tristram Shandy* where the writer's intent is to belie reader expectation. Readers can experience such surprise that they stop reading: writers, however, seldom surprise themselves to the same degree and stop writing.

Under likenesses, it was noted that the processes of writing and reading are characterized by the orchestration of such shared subprocesses as memory, cognition, language, and perception. One major subprocess, however, seems more active in the writing process than in the reading process: the neural-motor component. In writing, the production of a text is almost always a more physical activity. We include here the writer who voice-actuates a typewriter or word processor, who dictates and later revises, and even the paraplegic who blows on an alphabet board. Proficient, or mature, reading demands relatively less, often relying only on the hand to turn the page and the sweep of the eye across the visual data. What this difference might mean for the two processes is wholly speculative. Perhaps writing can be regarded as more "grounded" than reading in that it emanates organically from the body of the writer: the text one has written then possesses unique physical validity and perhaps even unique worth. It cannot be said that the absence of a motoric component makes reading more abstract since the making of a poem from a text represents its own unique form of highly specific personal knowledge.

The processes are not mutually embedded in the sense that we can read indefinitely without writing; we cannot long write without reading—that is, rereading what we have written. In 1969, Emig noted that, for the subjects in her study, a paragraph proved to be that unit at the end of which the writer stopped to reread. And in his 1977 interview for the *New York Review of Books*, Sartre stated that he had to give up writing when he became blind in his second eye and could no longer read at his own rhythm what he had just written. Atwell (1981) reported that both proficient and basic writers who could not read their texts while composing were adversely affected, but the more proficient less profoundly concerning the overall shape and direction of their texts.

Origins: Developmental Views

Developmentally, writing and reading share common origins, but with writing rather than reading the process that seems to develop earlier (Chomsky, 1971; Durkin, 1966; Durrell, 1966; Emig, 1982; Graves, 1978). What marker do scholars regard as the index that writing begins earlier than reading in the life of the child? Such otherwise divergent thinkers as Huey (1908), Mead (1934), and Vygotsky (1934, trans. 1978) claim that the gesture of the infant represents the beginnings of writing.

Vygotsky presents the fullest case, claiming that the gesture is "the initial visual sign that contains the child's future writing as an acorn contains the future oak." Gestures are writing in air, and written signs frequently are simply gestures that have been fixed. Early on, children shuttle between actual gestures and scribbles on paper that supplement this gestural representation. In fact, Vygotsky regards the child's first marks on paper developmentally as recorded gestures rather than as drawing in any true sense of that word. These marks on paper go through a series of evolutionary change, from undifferentiated marks through indicatory signs and symbolizing marks and scribbles to the drawing of little figures and pictures (pictographs) until the moment when the child realizes that one can draw not only things but speech. This recognition makes possible the gradual transformation of writing from a second-order symbolic act to a first-order symbolic act, from the mnemotechnic stage to the stage where one can deal with disembodied signs and symbols— to the stage, that is, of symbolic maturity. (Vygotsky also makes the case for symbolic play as the second link between gesture and written language.)

Drawing upon the work of these investigators as well as her own research, Birnbaum (1981) theorized that children's recognition of the meaning-making potential of their own scribbles is prerequisite to recognition of the meaning-making potential of others' texts. Therefore, interest in writing might precede interest in reading, although ability to read individual words might precede ability to handwrite legible words.

Jones and Hendrickson (1970); Altwerger and Y. Goodman (1978); Burke, Harste, and Woodward (1982); and DeFord (1980) are among those conducting a second strand of developmental inquiries under the rubric "print awareness," which they define as the ability of children to distinguish the salient features of written discourse from those of oral discourse. In these experimental studies, children as young as 2 years of age are demonstrating print awareness, a requisite obviously for both reading and writing. Jones and Hendrickson, examining how 3, 4, and 5 year olds attended to print on food product containers advertised on television and to titles of children's books read to them, found that the children were more familiar with print on the food containers than with titles of children's books; and that the children used such visual cues as colors, design, and accompanying pictures to aid them in correctly matching print to item. They suggest that children pass through developmental levels in learning written language. DeFord notes in her summaries of these studies:

> In the same way that young babies at six months are babbling, already having selected a repertoire of phonemes used in the language environment in which they live, so do writers begin to organize their world of print. This developmental process parallels oral language development and is initiated in the same way: through living and growing in a meaningful, print-oriented society. (p. 158)

A third strand of these inquiries into origins of literacy is into children's "invented spelling" and developing use of conventions. Read (1971) was the first researcher to examine the highly regular developmental sequence 3, 4, and 5 year old children follow as they invent and then modify a system of phonological rules that comes to approximate the system of standard American English orthography. Subsequent confirmation of his findings and the gradual internalization of written language conventions appear in the work of Bissex (1981), Calkins (1979), Chomsky (1975), Graves (1982), and Milz (1980).

Research on children's sense of story represents a fourth strand of research. As with the prior three, the generalization that obtains is that children's sense of story occurs far earlier than researchers had previously thought, beginning with recognition of its purpose. Halliday (1975), reviewing functions of language in his case study of his son, Nigel, states

> the child also uses language for creating a universe of his own, a world initially of pure sound, but which gradually turns into one of story and make believe and let's pretend, and ultimately into the realm of poetry and imaginative writing. (p. 20)

Birnbaum and Emig

As Applebee notes (1977), Nigel has begun this progression by the age of 15 months when he is still in what Halliday calls "Phase 1" of language development. This is a phase that precedes the acquisition of the lexicogrammatical system usually identified as the beginning of speech.

Applebee himself (1977) studied the child's adaptation of three narrative conventions when asked to "Tell me a story": 1) consistent past tense; 2) beginning with a formal opening (Once upon a time); and 3) ending with a conventional closing (and lived happily ever after). Seventy percent of the stories told by 2 year olds made use of at least one of theses three conventions; by the age of 5, nearly half the subjects made use of all three.

Mastery of more complex narrative features occurs later, however (Brown 1977):

> there is a significantly greater use of dialogue, and the beginning of complex plot forms with clear clausal links are being established. Yet the thematic center, including a climax tied to theme, is relatively underdeveloped and of little conscious concern to children until after nine years of age. (p. 358)

In a study of stories written by students in grades three through eight, Bartlett (1981) found a developmental sequence of narrative markers to begin stories and to introduce crises. She found that between fifth and sixth grade children abandon such minimal markers as the adverbial phrase ("One day. . .") and the indefinite article ("a boy. . .") and adopt more varied rhetorical devices to surmount these problems. Bartlett speculates that at this age the influence of linguistic experiences derived from reading begins to influence writing strategies.

Politics and the Two Processes

If recent research suggests that the reading and writing processes (albeit not mirror images) are related, then experiences in one may enhance growth in the other and their development may be intertwined. Therefore, it seems necessary for schools to focus equally (or at least equitably) on the two processes. Until recently in the United States, reading enjoyed status as the far preferred process of literacy. The status of reading revealed itself in many ways, from its weighting in the curriculum noted earlier, to preferential funding received from both private and public sources.

In *Balance the Basics: Let Them Write*, Graves (1978) inveighed against the imbalance:

> Nowhere else in the world does reading maintain such a hold on early learning. Although reading is valued in other countries, it is viewed more in the perspective of total communication.
>
> Our anxiety about reading is a national neurosis. Where else in the world are children scrutinized for potential failure in a subject area in the first two months of school—or even before they enter school? And our worst worries are fulfilled. Children fail.
>
> Concern about reading is today such a political, economic, and social force in American education that an imbalance in forms of communication is guaranteed from the start of a child's schooling. (p. 3).

Graves noted that the national predilection to value reading above writing, and the other language arts, was reflected in federal monies assigned to the two processes: "For every $3,000 spent on children's ability to receive information, $1 was spent on their power to send it in writing." Examining more closely the record of unsponsored and sponsored research and development for the years 1955 to 1972, Graves found the actual state of research into writing abysmal: only 156 studies on writing in the elementary grades were conducted; 84 percent of these were dissertations alone; senior faculty themselves conducted almost no research; 68 percent were classroom bound focusing on what teachers were doing.

> The research conducted on best methods for teachers was of the worst type. We took the science model of research and attempted to remove certain variables from their context to explain the two crafts, teaching and writing, by dismissing environments through statistics. (p. 917)

Despite a recent surge of interest into the processes of writing and writing instruction, the imbalance remains. Why? One compelling possibility is that writing is politically the more powerful process. Throughout history, reading and writing have been regarded as politically dangerous. Why else have slaves, prisoners, and other minorities and majorities been denied the opportunity to read as well as write?

But writing stays the far more worrisome and incendiary process. A reading citizen can come to comprehend and criticize societal mores as well as governmental acts and decisions. But only a citizen who elects to write can cause genuine trouble, can become the radical, the revolutionary. A reading citizen stays a client, a consumer of a culture; a writing citizen becomes its creator, or destroyer.

We are not suggesting that reading as a process in our culture has been overstressed; given the unique personal, aesthetic, and moral values adhering to reading, overvaluing reading is probably not possible. Like Graves, we are arguing instead for balance, for at least equal attention to writing. Writing is the enabling literacy; reading, the responsive literacy. To be wholly human requires that we be wholly literate—able to create as to respond.

References

Altwerger, B., & Goodman, Y. *Print awareness in preschool children: A working paper. A study of the development of literacy in preschool children.* Tucson, Arizona, 1981.

Anderson, R. *Schema directed processes in language comprehension.* Center for the Study of Reading Tech. Rep. 50. Urbana, Illinois: University of Illinois, July 1977.

Applebee, A. A sense of story. *Theory into Practice*, 1977, *16*, 342-347.

Atwell, M.A. The evolution of text: The interrelationship of reading and writing in the composing process. Unpublished dissertation, Indiana University, 1981.

Bartlett, E. Children's development of narrative. Paper presented at New York Linguistic Circle meeting, December 1981.

Bereiter, C. Developing in writing. In S. White & R. Tylers (Eds.), *Testing, teaching, and learning.* Washington, D.C.: National Institute of Education, 1979.

Birnbaum, J.C. The reading and composing behaviors of selected fourth and seventh grade students. Unpublished dissertation, Rutgers University, 1981.

Bissex, G. *Gnys at wrk.* Cambridge, Massachusetts: Harvard University Press, 1980.

Britton, J. *Language and learning.* London: Penguin Education, 1970.

Brown, G.H. Development of story in children's reading and writing. *Theory into Practice*, 1977, *16*, 357-362.

Brown, R. *Words and things.* New York: Academic Press, 1959.

Burke, C.L., Harste, J.C., & Woodward, V.A. Children's language and world: Initial encounters with print. In J. Langer & M. Smith-Burke (Eds.), *Reader meets author: Bridging the gap.* Newark, Delaware: International Reading Association, 1981.

Calkins, L. When children want to punctuate: Basic skills belong in context. Unpublished paper, University of New Hampshire, 1979.

Chomsky, C. Invented spelling in the open classroom. In von Raffles Engel (Ed.), *Word 27*, special issue of *Child Language Today*, 1975, 499-518.

Chomsky, C. Write first, read later. *Childhood Education*, 1971, *47*, 396-399.

Collins, C. The effect of writing experiences in the expressive mode upon the reading, self-esteem, attitudes and academic achievements of freshmen in a college reading course. Unpublished doctoral dissertation, Rutgers University, 1979.

Crews, R. A linguistic versus a traditional grammar program of effects on written sentence structure and comprehension. *Educational Leadership*, 1971, *5*, 145-149.

de Beaugrande, R. The processes of invention: Association and recombination. *College Composition and Communication*, 1979, *30*, 260-267.

DeFord, D. Young children and their writing. *Theory into Practice*, 1980, *19*, 157-162.

Dewey, J. *Art as experience.* New York: Capricorn Books, 1934. G.P. Putnam's Sons, 1958.

Durkin, D. *Children who read early: Two longitudinal studies.* New York: Teachers College Press, 1966.

Durrell, D. quoted in Graves, Donald. *Balance the basics: Let them write.* New York: Ford Foundation Report, 1978.

Eisner, E. The role of the arts in cognition and curriculum. *Phi Delta Kappan*, 1981, 48-52.

Emig, J. *The composing processes of twelfth graders* (1969). Urbana, Illinois: National Council of Teachers of English, 1971.

Emig, J. Nonmagical thinking: Presenting writing developmentally in schools. In C. Fredriksen & J. Dominic (Eds.), *The nature, development and teaching of written communication* (Vol. 2). Hillsdale, New Jersey: Erlbaum, 1982.

Evans, R.V. The effect of transformational simplification on the reading comprehension of selected high school students. *Journal of Reading Behavior*, 1972, *5*, 273-281.

Evans, R.V. The relationship between the reading and writing of syntactic structures. *Research in the Teaching of English*, 1979, *13*, 129-135.

Evanechko, P., Ollila, L., & Armstrong, R. An investigation of the relationship between children's performance in written language and their reading ability. *Research in the Teaching of English*, 1974, *8*, 315-325.

Flower, L. Writer based prose: A cognitive basis for problems in writing. *College English*, 1979, *41*, 19-37.

Gardner, H. *The shattered mind: The person after brain damage.* New York: Alfred A. Knopf, 1975.

Goodman, K.S. (Ed.). *The psycholinguistic nature of the reading process.* Detroit: Wayne State University Press, 1968.

Goodman, K.S., & Goodman, Y. Learning about psycholinguistic processes by analyzing oral reading. *Harvard Educational Review*, 1977, *47*, 317-333.

Graves, D. *Balance the basics: Let them write.* New York: Ford Foundation Report, 1978.

Graves, D.H. Bullock and beyond: Research on the writing process. In F.R.A. Davis & R.P. Parker, Jr. (Eds.), *Teaching for literacy: Reflections on the Bullock report.* New York: Agathon Press, 1978.

Graves, D.H. Children's writing: Research directions and hypotheses based upon an examination of the writing process of seven year old children. Unpublished dissertation, State University of New York at Buffalo, 1973.

Graves, D.H. Patterns of child control of the writing process. In R.D. Walshe (Ed.), *Donald Graves in Australia.* Exeter, New Hampshire: Heinemann, 1982.

Graves, D. Research update. A new look at writing. *Language Arts*, 1980, *57*, 913-918.

Halliday, M.A.K. *Learning how to mean: Explorations in the development of language.* London: Edward Arnold, 1975.

Huey, E.B. *The psychology and pedagogy of reading* (1908). Cambridge, Massachusetts: MIT Press, 1978.

Hughes, T.O. *Sentence-combining: A means of increasing reading comprehension*, 1975. (ED 112 421)

Iser, W. *The implied reader: Patterns of communication from Bunyon to Beckett.* Baltimore and London: Johns Hopkins Press, 1975.

Jones, M., & Hendrickson, N. Recognition by preschool children of advertised products and bookcovers. *Journal of Home Economics*, 1970, *4*, 263-267.

Kelly, G. *A theory of personality.* New York: W.W. Norton, 1955.

Kuntz, M.H. The relationship between written syntactic attainment and reading ability in seventh grade. Doctoral dissertation, University of Pittsburgh, 1975.

Langer, S.K. *Feeling and form.* New York: Charles Scribner & Sons, 1953.

Langer, S.K. *Philosophy in a new key: A study in the symbolism of reason, rite, and art* (3rd Ed.). Cambridge, Massachusetts: Harvard University Press, 1956.

Lazdowski, W.F. Determining reading grade levels from analysis of written composition. Doctoral dissertation, New Mexico State University, 1976.

Loban, W. *Language development, kindergarten through grade twelve.* Urbana, Illinois: National Council of Teachers of English, 1976.

Mead, G. *Mind, self, and society.* University of Chicago Press, 1934.

Milz, V. First graders can write: Focus on communication. *Theory into Practice,* 1980, 179-185.

Nystrand, M. Using readability research to investigate writing. *Research in the Teaching of English,* 1979, *13,* 231-242.

Obenchain, J. *Sequential steps to effective writing: A programmed approach with direction of reading skills and literature appreciation.* Arlington, Virginia: Cooper-Trent, 1972.

Page, W.D. The author and the reader in writing and reading. *Research in the Teaching of English,* 1974, *8,* 170-182.

Perl, S. The composing processes of unskilled college writers. *Research in the Teaching of English,* 1979, *13,* 317-336.

Pianko, S. The composing acts of college freshmen writers: A description. Unpublished doctoral dissertation, Rutgers University, 1977.

Polanyi, M. *The tacit dimension.* New York: Doubleday, 1966.

Pringle, I., & Freedman, A. Writing in the college years: Some indices of growth. Paper presented at the annual meeting of the National Council of Teachers of English, San Francisco, 1979.

Read, C. Preschool children's knowledge of English phonology. *Harvard Educational Review,* 1971, *23,* 17-38.

Read, C. *Why writing is not the inverse of reading for young children.* NIE Conference on Writing, 1977.

Rosenblatt, L.M. *Literature as exploration* (1938). New York: Noble and Noble, 1968.

Rosenblatt, L.M. *The reader, the text, the poem: The transactional theory of the literary work.* Carbondale, Illinois: Southern Illinois University Press, 1979.

Ruddell, R.B. Psycholinguistic implications for a system of communication mode. In K.S. Goodman & J.T. Fleming (Eds.), *Psycholinguistics and the teaching of reading.* Newark, Delaware: International Reading Association, 1969.

Sartre, Jean-Paul. Interview with Michel Contat. *New York Review of Books,* 1978, 10.

Shanahan, R. The impact of writing instruction on learning to read. *Reading World,* 1980, *19,* 357-368.

Smith, F. *Psycholinguistics and reading.* New York: Holt, Rinehart & Winston, 1973.

Smith, F. *Understanding reading.* New York: Holt, Rinehart & Winston, 1970.

Smith, F. *Writers and writing.* New York: Holt, Rinehart & Winston, 1982.

Smith, W.L. The effect of transformed syntactic structures on reading. In C. Braun (Ed.), *Language, reading, and the communication process.* Newark, Delaware: International Reading Association, 1971.

Stotsky, S.L. Sentence-combining as a curricular activity: Its effect on written language development and reading comprehension. *Research in the Teaching of English,* 1975, *9,* 30-71.

Takahashi, B.L. Comprehension of written syntactic structures by good readers and slow readers. Unpublished master's thesis, Rutgers University, 1975.

Vygotsky, L.S. The prehistory of written language. In M. Cole, V. John-Steiner, S. Scribner, & E. Souberman (Eds.), *Mind in society: The development of psychological processes* (A.R. Luria, Trans.). Cambridge, Massachusetts: Harvard University Press, 1978.

Wolfe, R.F. An examination of the effects of teaching a reading vocabulary upon writing vocabulary in student composition. Doctoral dissertation, University of Maryland, 1975.

Young, R., Becker, A.L., & Pike, K.L. *Rhetoric: Discovery and change.* New York: Harcourt Brace Jovanovich, 1970.

Writing: What For?

Nancy Martin
University of London

What do students in school learn from writing that lasts into adult life? The answer is bound to be speculative. How much adults write is a social and cultural matter related to how they view writing and to what extent different social groups need it for practical purposes. What we can say with certainty is that in the western world everyone feels that to be illiterate (unable to sign your name or write at all) is a matter of shame and secrecy. Beyond this, I would guess that the majority don't write anything much, and regard it as a risky chore to be avoided whenever possible.

This was not always so. In medieval Europe, for instance, education was strictly vocational and it was no shame to be illiterate. Reading and writing were left to professionals while other people got on with their practicalities. Writing in particular was a menial task and was chiefly undertaken by professional scriveners who carried out all the writing people required—for a fee, of course.

Reading and writing, which we think of as complementary, grew up under separate auspices, and were taught separately for strictly practical purposes. Reading was in the hands of the church and always associated with singing the various parts of the church services. Writing was coupled with arithmetic and taught by the scriveners (who were also accountants and valuers); it had a lay origin and no status.

After the Renaissance and the development of printing, writing became part of the curriculum in the lay schools but, even then, it was introduced with the greatest care. Schoolmasters were afraid of opposition from the Master Scribes and had uneasy consciences, said a contemporary writer. The authorities did not find the problem easy to solve; for instance, an edict from the French High Court in 1661 stated, "Scribes may have printed books or texts to teach spelling but they must not on any account teach reading!" (Restrictive practices by Unions then as now.)

I have given these few historical details to illustrate the tenacious and indissoluble link between schooling and the practicalities of adult life. I don't think people's views are very different today, except that our society believes people should be literate; but the uses they see in writing are restricted and are limited to vocational and practical needs.

There is, of course, the other historical thread which sprang from the Hellenistic tradition and was embodied in the curriculum of the old grammar schools with their notions of a liberal education which maintained that acquaintance with the best models of classical writing and thought would mold students into educated individuals. This notion of a liberal education appears to run counter to the vocational direction, but even here there was a social-cum-vocational element in that educated persons were products of their class and demonstrated it by learning many useless things from a vocational point of view. All this seems to present a continuing tradition of focus on the future—on the adult life of students.

But a different perspective gradually emerged. I want to draw attention to just two aspects of these changes. First, the increasing mobility of labor means that society is no longer stratified enough to predict what people will need (the barrow boy to the business tycoon syndrome) but, in any case, so much of what we learn in school won't pass a test of future usefulness. It is hard to pinpoint what has lasted for each of us from our educations. What do we remember of all those lessons, all that information? Or what kind of things? Not very much, I suspect, though there was the case of the dampproofer who sat in my

Martin

house recently and talked at great length about *Great Expectations.* "I could tell you everything that happened in that book," he said, "but I went into building; I suppose I learned there's a lot in books, though I don't read them. It's all there if you want it."

Second, and most important, the focus in education began to shift from the future to the here and now. People began to think there were things appropriate and valuable for youth that might have nothing directly to do with their futures, but which were indirectly important and without which the children's futures were diminished. In this context I think of games and play, of fairy stories and fiction, and of love and demonstrated affection. To these, I would add writing. We take these views so for granted that only a look at history reveals how revolutionary this particular change is.

Thus, to answer the question about what of school writing lasts into adult life, it is necessary to consider what writing can do for students, regardless of the narrow limits of adult writing. Furthermore, the growing volume of work coming from many disciplines on the significance of language in learning means that teachers today are concerned both with the struggle for basic literacy, and with the development of thinking (of which basic literacy is a starting point). Generally speaking, teachers realize that if basic literacy is seen as the end rather than the means, children's entry into the universe of discourse (which shapes, and is shaped by, thinking) is diminished, if not denied. It seems to me that the potential of writing is still beyond the horizon of most people's view—writing still rests in the hard utilitarian shell of its origin.

I am going to focus, therefore, on aspects of writing in school because that is where writing is potentially freest of vocational drag and (potentially) most powerful in shaping thinking. I am going to explore two particular aspects which have been my concern in the past three years: I refer to them as *models* and *contexts.*

First, models. We do not fully realize how much we all learn about nearly everything from seeing people do things in the customary way; perhaps we rely too much on direct instruction and not enough on encounters with models. The term *model* is not used in its common meaning of something to be consciously imitated, but as something whose use and form are recognized by repeated encounters—not specially noticed or deliberately imitated. I am talking about "literary" experience—encounters with various forms of the written language which act as unconscious models to young writers. Lyons (1964) suggested there are "mutually maintained conventions and presuppositions" which govern our understanding of particular types of linguistic behavior (telling a story, philosophizing, buying, selling, praying, writing a novel). If we ask how these mutually understood conventions are acquired, we can say only that experience of encountering them is major and, from their earliest years, children are busy sorting out these conventions and "rules of use" which tell them what is what in the world of print.

I shall try to illustrate this process by two examples, one from beginners in nursery school and one from children at the end of primary school who can write and read and who are beginning to try out different "voices" in their writing. The first example comes from an observation while working with a gifted nursery school teacher. It is a record of a conversation between the teacher and Andrew, aged 3 years, 11 months. Andrew is investigating stories (Martin, 1976).

(When Andrew came into the office his teacher was entering recent happenings into the log book.)

Andrew: What are you writing?

Miss E: Some of the interesting things that have happened here in the nursery.

Andrew: Tell me them.

Miss E: This one says, "Mrs Taylor and Mrs. Shotton visited the nursery during the afternoon session to see the climbing frame and make arrangements for its removal."

Andrew: What did they want to look at it for? Drew says they are going to take it away on a truck.

Miss E: I'm hoping so. It's very rusty and dangerous for you to use. That's why I asked Mrs. Shotton to come and see it. Then I wrote all about it in this book.

Andrew: Read some more.

Miss E: "The nursery school closed for the October holidays."

Andrew: The writing's different. Why?

Miss E: Mrs Tindale wrote these two pages. You see, I wasn't feeling well and had to stay at home.

Andrew: Is that in?

Miss E: Yes, here it is.

Andrew: What are the numbers for?

Miss E: That is the date. It tells the exact day it happened.

Andrew: Is it all real? Is it a true story?

Miss E: Everything in here is true. I write down only the things that actually happen.

Andrew: Do you ever write down about the boys and girls?

Miss E: Often. Let's find some. This one tells about the day we all went to Stanley Zoo. Here is one about Diane and the day she cut her eye and had to be taken to the hospital.

Andrew: It's a nice storybook. Why have you never read it to us?

Miss E: I'm sorry I didn't think of it. Perhaps you could even help to write it. You could let me know all the important things that happen, and I'll be sure to write them all down in this special book.

Andrew: I'll bet you won't put it with the other books though.

Miss E: No. This is a special book so it has to stay in a special place—on my cupboard.

Andrew: Are all books real? They're not, are they? Some of them are. The one about the farm and the car book and the seaside, they're real. But it's hard to know. Is *Monkey Island* real? That's my favorite, except for one thing. Mrs. Stewart says the boy hasn't got a name in the book. But Zippo (the monkey) has. Do you think it's a true story?

Miss E: I'm not sure. You go and get the book and we'll see if it says so inside.

Andrew: (returning with the book) It's not a true story. I asked in there. I don't know whether it's my favorite any more.

In this incident, Andrew is trying to "place" the school log in the context of his experience of stories. He has not hitherto connected stories printed in a book with a person writing with a pen. He also recognizes that it is all true and judges it "a nice story. Why have you never read it to us?" Then he reassesses his favorite story because it is not true. At this stage he is not experienced enough in the "conventions and rules of use" to be sure when a story is true and whether to incorporate it into his growing picture of life as it is, so the "truth" criterion is all important. Later when he has more experience with stories and can recognize them, he will not have to be so concerned about the "Is it true?" issue and can enjoy them as fiction.

My second example is more complex and speculative. It consists of short excepts from the writing of a group of 10 year olds about a pond dipping expedition. I was interested in the various models they seemed to be drawing on as they incorporated these different voices into their writing. Some seem to be deliberately trying different ways of speaking, while others are still at the stage where they put down what first comes to mind, very much as they would speak; i.e., their models are still the spoken language in spite of good experiences with books and writing. There was a common starting point in the shared expedition and the topic (but no title) given, but there was no expectation of a common finishing point, or that all would include the same things. The reverse was true. The children clearly expected they would proceed in their own directions in their own ways. This had two consequences: One, they do not edit out the expressive features of their writing which articulate their subjective response to the life of the pond; and two, they are sensitive to the language encountered and draw on a variety of models from books, from their teachers, and from conversation. However, this freedom to move about as they wish within the subject matter does mean that their selection of items is eclectic, depending on what catches their interests. Until they begin to use generalizations systematically, what they write inevitably has this random character.

Lyn wrote:

> Do you know what this is? A pond is the answer (colored picture). Fish (colored drawing). Water Spider (colored drawing). These are just two of the things that live in the pond. Of course there are more things. A fish breathes through its mouth and can only live in water like we would die if we were put in water for a long while and could not come out. A water spider lives in a bubble of air underneath the water. It can also run across the water without getting its feet wet. . . . (Martin, 1971)

This is very much as Lyn would speak, and she tells which items caught her interest.

Robert Farmer's piece is very different. He starts with a generalization but doesn't make use of it to structure his piece which must have literary experience in the background of its consciously bookish and humorous tone.

> A pond can be anywhere, behind trees, by the railway, almost anywhere you think of there is likely to be a pond. When you have found a pond, unknown to you and me the thousands of little creatures go into exile. They hide under stones, under weeds, and in the mud. . . .An interesting creature is the Caddis fly larva. This is an interesting creature because it is a tasty meal for any animal who feels a little peckish. . . .

Martin also feels it is appropriate to begin with a generalization:

> A pond is a small lake filled by vegertion (I think "vergertion" means plants *and* animals to him). Tadpoles, sticklebacks and minowes are some of the most common ones. . . .

Unlike most of the children, Martin does not choose the most interesting creatures to describe, but follows up his second generalization about the most common ones. He continues with a third generalization which he develops:

> Dragonflys are the enemy of most insects in the pond. When they are young they prowl around like cats to catch insects.

He then goes on to describe the family life of sticklebacks. You can see in this account the beginnings of the adult pattern of weaving in and out of the general and particular.

Neil headed his piece "Science." A pointer perhaps to how he thought about it—yet another model? and a familiar one.

> In the pond there are many different kinds of creatures. Fish are a certain shape so they can get through the water fast. They are said to be streamlined. It is best when pond dipping to put plant eating insects in one tank and meat eating insects in another. Caddis flies make their houses with anything they can get their feelers on....

Although he has the scientific voice with its impersonal phrases, his piece lacks any structuring in relation to the general statements he begins by using. He is imitating a model without *using* it.

Robert Lim seems to be drawing on similar models but uses them to bring together his book knowledge and his own observations. An example of a writer using his writing to think with?

> A pond is full of life. A whole city in miniature may exist in a pond. The animals in the pond are either carnivorous or vegetarian.... Of all the things that live in the pond the Caddis fly larva is the one with the best camouflage. It makes a kind of shed out of the substance around it.
>
> The water spider has an ingenious method of breathing under water. He makes his den and then he brings down air bubbles in his hind legs!
>
> The fish breathe by breathing in water and then extracting its properties of oxygen by means of a type of grid (drawing)....

His first paragraph shows generalizations being used to structure all the items in the paragraph. I think by "city in miniature" he is getting at the idea of an underwater community with its carnivores and vegetarians, and with carnivores around some of the creatures will need camouflage. Then he goes on to describe methods of breathing. His items are not random; to be concerned with methods of breathing under water implies a hierarchy of

Martin

related ideas which is altogether different from Lyn's egocentrically interested report that water spiders can run across water without getting their feet wet.

I think a pedagogical point arises from this loosely graded set of writings. When children are free to select and order as they wish, they are also free to draw consciously—or unconsciously—on the language resources that are in their inner ears from reading, from television, and from their teachers. If they are given a particular model or way of writing, they cannot draw freely on these resources and cannot attempt to shape what they write, and shaping in referential writing is thinking itself. It follows that teaching, in writing, should play a secondary or consultative role. We should rely more on encounters with many and varied models.

This raises the question of what models are influential. I think the answer is those models which children can make use of. Where children have special interests they make use of surprising models; in more general terms, the most influential models are those children can use because they have something in common with their language and viewpoints. Literature-stories, poems, and plays mean more because they are forms of personal language. It is all most children can do to see the world and describe it from their individual points of view. Often they can see how it looks to one other person, but this is different from seeing things from the viewpoint of people in general, i.e. the impersonal viewpoint. Beyond this, the individual viewpoint encompasses inner emotions and events and intimations which cannot be expressed explicitly; the symbolic renderings of experience which we call stories and poems enable us to find a form of expression for these intangibles. This is true for all of us, but particularly important for children who can only talk and read about these things through the "allegories" of literature.

Fortunately, stories and poems abound in most schools but opportunities for children to encounter good transactional writing are more limited, especially in secondary schools where a variety of models is not usually part of the picture of subject teaching. In any case, good transactional writings are hard to come by. People are not too concerned about the quality of informational writing. It is gauged on different criteria: Is the information accurate? Is it an appropriate selection? Is it presented in a way that is easy to memorize? All of these are important, but quality of writing (whatever that means in this case) is more significant than is perhaps realized since so much of language development seems to be a matter of acquiring the voices of the available models.

The way in which language is extended is a mysterious process, part of which seems to lie in repeated encounters with "models", part in writers' conscious or unconscious use of their own versions of these "models", and ultimately in their commitment to what they are doing when they write. I think commitment is a function of intention. I now want to consider what scope for students' intentions there is in school environments, i.e., look at one example of contexts for writing, and try to assess its significance for student intentions.

In West Australia I was invited to report on English teaching and learning in the Government High Schools, and I set out to look specifically at the scope for intentions that different school contexts might provide. I made case studies of nine schools and looked particularly at the evidence from the writing and from interviews with students. What I have to say here comes from a school where I studied in detail the writing done in two senior classes (16 to 17 years) in the context of the beliefs and practices of the six teachers comprising the English department (Martin, 1980).

What I found substantiated what some of us are beginning to think about commitment and the place of intention in writing. I had two questions in mind which were hypotheses arising from the work we did in England on the Writing across the Curriculum Project (Martin, 1976). First, could we find classes where all the students, or at least the majority, learned to write well (excluding those few able and committed students who turn up in most classes and provide the material for most anthologies of student writing)? Second, would such a general level of writing ability be related to some consensus of beliefs and attitudes among their teachers which related not only to English but to education and to life? (Both hypotheses were positing something about social and intellectual relationships which extended beyond the individual.)

In these two classes we found good quality writing from all the students. The range of ability was wide. The writings were varied, competent, honest, reflective, experimental, and highly individual.

The most powerful part of the context for the writings was the social and intellectual climate created by the English teachers. Central to this climate were the teachers' convictions about the need for face-to-face talk irrespective of status, so that staff and students might understand and modify one another's intentions. The English staff room (and students could always be found there) was a focusing point in that it was an ongoing seminar for the discussion of ideas. All that the teachers said and did asserted their beliefs in nonhierarchical relationships and mutual respect. In this context, trust was a "given" and writing flourished. It seems significant that assessments were made only for work geared to writing for public examinations.

In addition to the social beliefs (and to what I can only call the political beliefs) which caused these teachers to create this environment for learning, there were the teachers' ideas and beliefs about language and literature. These were explicitly discussed in the ongoing talk with their students and were directly realized in the options for writing. Nothing was prescribed (i.e. the option of "a topic of your own choosing" was always included) and what was suggested embodied the teachers' theoretical knowledge about language, education, and literature. In summary, these were:

1. The importance of creative writing in developing personal growth and general writing ability.
2. The value of personal reflective writing addressed to a particular audience in the form of a continuing journal.
3. The value of long term, extended assignments rather than essays or short pieces.
4. A continuous background of reading and discussion of literature.
5. In transactional writing, the importance of first hand experience as the means by which a student can enter

and make sense of secondary experience (i.e. book knowledge).

Thus, as Britton (1980) suggested, there was commitment to a relationship and commitment to learning, these being rooted in transactions between people who experience themselves as autonomous and mutually respecting party equals, at least in the right to speak and be heard if not in knowledge and wisdom.

I want to conclude with a question about the relationship between the creative talent which is given shape in children's writing, and the society in which they become adults. The context for what Hughes (1975) says was the introduction he wrote to a national literary competition for children between the ages of 6 and 16. The competition has occurred annually for twenty years and some 50,000 children enter each year. Hughes wrote:

> The talent is so abundant that it is difficult to stabilize one's attitude toward it. Ought we to think of it as something quite natural but also— as a rule—quite fleeting, like teenage beauty? Or ought we to think of it as an overwhelming supply of potential real ability, which somehow— because of educational and social conditions—we are failing to catch and develop?
>
> Writing ability is not a freakish knack, connected to nothing in particular. In any social group, the imaginative writers are the most visible indicators of the level and energy and type of the imagination and other vital mental activities in the whole group. What everybody in the group shares in a hidden way, or needs to share, comes to expression in the writer. . . .
>
> It has often been said that children's writing is not simply adult writing in the larval stage. . . . The differences between children's sensibility and adult sensibility are obviously big and real. . . . theirs is still very much the naked process of apprehension, far less conditioned than ours, far more fluid and alert, far closer to the real laws of its real nature. . . . Losing that sort of exposed nakedness, we gain in confidence and in mechanical efficiency on our chosen front, but we lose in curiosity, in perception, in the original, wild, no-holds-barred approach to problems. . . .
>
> Looking over these pieces, anyone must wonder: What happens to all this talent? One of the curious facts about this competition, which has now been going on for so long, is that so very few have emerged in their adult life as writers. . . . Perhaps it merely confirms that children's writing is, for one reason or another, a thing apart. One wonders, however, whether the reason might not be a sinister one. . . . The statistics become even more curious when we remember that among the individuals who do later become outstanding writers, very few show more than a rudimentary talent up to their adolescence. . . . the

suspicion remains that we are talking about an unhappy, not to say disastrous, state of affairs, where this immense biological oversupply of precocious ability is almost totally annihilated before it can mature. What is the future of a society, we wonder, that manages to lobotomize its talent in this way? Can anything at all be done about it?

Obviously, a competition for writing, even one as big as this, can do very little. What it does, perhaps, is promote the creative mood in schools. . . . A creative mood can be induced in any group, just as a demoralized mood or a destructive mood can be induced. . . . What is not so easy is to imagine how the creative mood can be induced in any part of society outside schools. The inability of creative talent, at present, to survive leaving school, is perhaps, one visible aspect of what must be a destructive mood in society as a whole. A self-destructive mood that shuts down imagination and energy. It is not the only visible aspect, but it is, properly considered, the most horrifying—a massacre of the innocents with a vengence.

References

Aries, P. *Centuries of childhood.* New York: Vintage Books, Random House, 1962, 288-298.

Britton, J. Keynote address. Conference on college composition and communication, Washington, D.C., 1980.

Hughes, T. Foreword. *Children as writers 2.* London: Heinemann, 1975.

Lyons J. *Structural semantics.* Blackwell, 1964.

Martin, N. Encounters with models. *English in Education,* 1976, *19.*

Martin, N. What are they up to? *Children using language.* Oxford University Press, 1971.

Martin, N. *The Martin report.* Perth, Western Australia: Department of Education, Western Australia, 1980.

Martin, N., D'Arcy, P., Newton, B., & Parker, R. *Writing and learning across the curriculum.* London: Ward Lock, 1976, 11-16.

The Reading Transaction: What For?

Louise M. Rosenblatt
Princeton, New Jersey

To be asked the question, "Reading, what for?" in the context of a conference on young children's use of language is a reminder of the importance of underlying theory. In a developmental framework, it is customary to describe the adult stage toward which children are presumably progressing. The picture of the adult or skilled reader is invoked, not in order to impose the adult pattern on children's early reading but, rather, in order to derive developmental, or directional, criteria. Unfortunately, it is all too possible to have short term successes in the teaching of reading, while using methods and materials that turn the youngsters away from growth toward our long term goals. Hence, I understand the need for the question "Reading, what for?" to be answered in terms of the adult reader.

Reading is a relationship between a human being and a text, and the purpose of that activity involves the whole person. To ask what kinds of readers we hope our young people will become is to ask what kinds of human beings we hope they will become. It is easy to suggest negative answers to such questions. For example, Auden's "The Unknown Citizen" (1945) begins

> He was found by the bureau of statistics to be
> One against whom there was no official complaint,

and lists among his virtues

> He was fully sensible to the advantages of the installment plan
> And had everything necessary to the modern man,

        A phonograph, a radio, a car and a frigidaire.
        The researchers of public opinion are content
        That he held the proper opinions for the time of year....

and ends

        And our teachers report that he never interfered with their education.
        Was he free? Was he happy? The question is absurd:
        Had anything been wrong, we should certainly have heard.

For the development of that kind of reader in that kind of society, a minimum concept of literacy, a listing of skills, might possibly suffice. If we envision the ideal of a humane, democratic society composed of mature people, we cannot simply list advanced high-level skills. We must draw upon abstractions such as to be "free," to be "happy." We must speak of our hope for people with a sense of personal identity, who reject a life of dehumanized uniformity, who seek an expansion of knowledge and awareness, and who possess the imagination to feel themselves part of the human community. In more usual terms, they are capable of fulfilling their responsibilities as members of families and as citizens, capable of participating in the intellectual and artistic life of our society. This assumes also the ability to reflect critically on their own values, their own world.

    Reading can in many ways serve the needs and foster the development of such people. Reading is "for" the knowledge, the experience, and the wisdom that the printed word makes possible for us, giving us communication with other minds across time and space, enabling us to share in their thought and their worlds. Our libraries are overflowing with the great heritage of works of the past; the avalanche of new publications justifies talk of a "knowledge explosion"; rising levels of education and leisure arouse hopes of increasing recourse to the arts, especially literature. But in this troubled century, we cannot point complacently to our great wealth encased in books. Their potentialities for good or evil remain moot, until we see in what kinds of relationships with readers these texts are brought to a "life beyond life."

    The question "What for?" is asked, consciously or unconsciously, by every reader encountering a text. Ultimately, there are as many answers as there are individual personalities, stages of development, and changing needs and interests. Yet this matter of purpose seems most often neglected in the theory and teaching of reading. Models of the reading process typically focus on cognition (Williams, 1971, pp. 7-142, 145). They rarely include motivation, and even then in a very generalized sense. The reader's attitude toward reading in general is very important. I am concerned, however, with the way in which purpose affects the actual process: the actions, procedures, or strategies of the reader during the reading event. I shall deal here only with the evocation of meaning; matters such as validity of interpretation and evaluation have been treated elsewhere (Rosenblatt, 1969, 1976, 1978).

Reading as Transaction

"Transaction" underlines my rejection of the epistemological dualism that would place the human being against nature as two separate or autonomous entities. Current ecological views of the human being in a two-way relationship with nature (Bateson, 1979; Toulmin, 1972), and current philosophy of science (Weizsäcker, 1980), with its recognition of the observer as an explicit factor in any observation or proposition, illustrate the transactional concept. Dewey (1896) reacted early against the stimulus-response view of the organism passively receiving the stimulus, and showed that, in a sense, the organism seeks out the stimuli to which it responds. As "interaction" suggested the dualism which he had long opposed, Dewey, in *Knowing and the Known* (1949), chose "transaction" to indicate a two-way, reciprocal relationship; thus "knowing" assumes a transaction between a knower and a known.

Transaction especially seems to be needed for a description of the act of reading. Reading is always a particular event, involving a particular reader, a particular item of the environment—a text, at a particular time, under particular circumstances. A person becomes a reader by virtue of a relationship with a text. A text is merely ink on paper, until some reader (if only the author)[1] evokes meaning from it. The transactional theory resists the formalist tendency to concentrate on the text as all-important and the reader as passive, and also avoids the alternative extremism of some recent "subjective" literary theorists who see the reader as all-important and the text as passive or secondary. Reader and text are mutually essential to the transaction; meaning happens during the transaction between the reader and the text.

Dynamics of Language

The reader's give and take with the text reflects the transactional nature of all language. It cannot be conceived simply as a code, a language, existing apart from parole, the linguistic acts of individual human beings (Saussure, 1916). Language is socially-generated and socially-acquired, a public system of communication. As Bruner (1977) phrases it, "In contemporary jargon, language is never to be understood as context independent." But it is easily forgotten that language is always individually internalized. One can understand why psychologists, despite their theoretical break with behaviorism, tend to persist in old experimental methods that deal mainly with public utterances. Equally essential is a conceptualization of the processes by which the individual participates in the public system.

The view of language that stems mainly from William James (1890) provides such a matrix for thinking about the process of reading. His brilliant metaphor of the stream of thought or consciousness (which now typically serves as a point of departure for cognitive psychologists emerging from the behaviorist interlude) encompasses not only ideas but "every form of consciousness indiscriminately"—sensations, images, precepts and concepts, states or qualities of states, feelings of relations, feelings of tendency. We sense our bodily selves as the seat of our thinking: for example, James (1890, pp. 245-246) suggests that we compare our internal states when we look at a tree stump and think of it as a chair, and when we think of it as a table. Such inner dynamics are present, he asserts, whether we think of the objects our words point to, or of the relationships among them:

> There is not a conjunction or a preposition, and hardly an adverbial phrase, syntactic form, or inflection of voice, in human speech, that does not express some shading or other of relation which we at some moment actually feel to exist between the larger objects of our thought. If we speak objectively, it is the real relations that appear revealed; if we speak subjectively, it is the stream of consciousness that matches each of them by an inward coloring of its own. . . . We ought to say a feeling of *and*, a feeling of *if*, a feeling of *but*, and a feeling of *by*, quite as readily as we say a feeling of *blue* or a feeling of *cold*.

Vygotsky (1962) also postulates the existence of a "dynamic system of meaning, in which the affective and the intellectual unite." He contrasts referential meaning and "sense":

> The sense of a word. . .is the sum of all the psychological events aroused in our consciousness by the word. It is a dynamic, fluid, complex whole, which has several zones of unequal stability. Meaning is only one of the zones of sense, the most stable and precise zone. A word acquires its sense from the context in which it appears; in different context, it changes its sense. The dictionary meaning of a word is no more than a stone in the edifice of sense, no more than a potentiality that finds diversified realization in speech. (p. 146)

This view of language is carried further by Werner and Kaplan (1963) in their study of the development of language and the expression of thought. We see the infant engaged in active sensory-motor exploration or transaction with the environment, internalizing "a primordial matrix composed of affective, interoceptive, postural, imaginal elements" (p. 18). From this, an innerdynamic or form-building or schematizing activity carries on the twin process of shaping both a sense of an external object or referent and a symbolic or linguistic vehicle and establishing a semantic correspondence between them. A word and its referent acquire meaning when they are linked to the same internal, organismic, state.

Thus the child's early vocables are shown as referring to a complex inner state corresponding to a total situation. "Early vocables are evoked by total happenings and are expressive not only of references to an event external to the child, but also reflect the child's attitudes, states, reactions" (p. 141). Development into two-vocable utterances and beyond depends on differentiation of reference, a process of delimitation and specification. The child must learn to sort out the various elements of the organismic state associated with a situation and must learn to distinguish between the referential, the external object or situation designated by the word, and the inner state, the attitudes and associations, linked with it. "With the progression toward the use of conventional [linguistic] forms, the inner form of the symbol (the connotational dynamics) becomes more and more *covert* in character—carried by 'inner gestures,' 'imagery,' 'postural-affective sets,' 'feelings,' etc." (p. 238). Increasing distance between these two aspects of meaning—the word and the inner state—does not imply a rupture between them, since this would deprive the word of its meaning and it would degenerate into a mere noise or mark. Even the referential aspect remains anchored to its organismic matrix; i.e., cognition is always accompanied by a qualitative or affective element, no matter how much, in some circumstances this element is ignored (Dewey, 1963).

Halliday (1975, 1978) has helped us to see the child's earliest vocalizations as a process of "learning to mean"; the child develops a sense of the different functions of language through a set of personal utterances, before assimilating the linguistic system of the environment. Yet Halliday's list of functions does not fully take care of the aspect we have been stressing—the attitudes and qualitative states bonded to verbal symbols. The two approaches seem needed, to account for both the public and personal functions of language.

Selective Attention in Reading

Given the view of language sketched thus far, it becomes possible to look more closely at the reading process. The assertion that the reading transaction involves the whole person takes on fuller import. The reader brings to the text the internalized sum, the accumulation or memory of all such psychological events, such past organismic encounters with language and the world. In the reading transaction, the words of the text may be said to activate elements of memory, to stir up the organismic state linked to the words and their referents. We must keep in mind that this potentially includes not only those aspects that circumscribe the public referents or objects to which the verbal symbols point but, also the personal referents—sensuous, affective, imaginal, and associative. Thus, the evocation of meaning from the text requires a selecting-out from the reservoir of thought and feeling, the acceptance of some elements into the center of attention, and the relegation of others to the periphery of awareness.

"Selective attention" is James's term (1890) for such sorting-out activity, an often-neglected concept basic to his idea of the stream of consciousness. "Consciousness," he tells us, "is always more interested in one part of its object than another, and welcomes or rejects or chooses, all the while." This results in the "selection of some [elements of the inner stream] and the suppression of the rest, by the reinforcing and inhibiting agency of attention." This "choosing activity" is central to thinking, and hence central to reading, which is a form of thinking in transaction with a text.

Reading consists of a continuing stream of choices on the reader's part. As the reader approaches the text, there is the need to develop guides for the selective process, guides that set up expectations and narrow the range of options from which to choose. Just as in the sequence of verbal symbols the article *a* suggests the syntactic category from which to choose the meaning of the next word, so the reader seeks cues to the formation of a guiding semantic principle—tentative, open to constant revision— that will guide the process of selective attention. As the verbal symbols activate areas of consciousness, the reader selects out and focuses attention on those elements that suggest a tentative framework that narrows the range of further choices, which again set up certain expectations, as a structure or meaning is developed. If expectations are inappropriate to subsequent verbal symbols in the text, revision of the guiding principle of selection, or perhaps a complete rereading, occurs. Selective attention thus serves the choosing, structuring, synthesizing activity which produces meaning.

The Efferent and the Aesthetic

The most decisive act of selective attention still remains to be defined. The general intention to make meaning out of the verbal symbols, though necessary, is not sufficient for a fully successful reading. The *kind* of meaning must be delimited. Either before the encounter with the text, or early in the reading event, the reader must select a general stance, a mental set, toward the internal states that will be activated by the pattern of words.

Every linguistic act we have seen encompasses both public and private elements—the general terms I have used to include aspects variously referred to as cognitive and affective, referential and emotive, denotative and connotative. The reader must choose the purpose, the mental set, that will determine the relative degrees of attention to be bestowed on the public and private aspects of the field of consciousness activated by the words. I term this the reader's choice of a predominant "stance" appropriate to his purpose. This will direct the whole selective process.

One part of the continuum of potential stances covers the mental set I term the "efferent" stance, from the Latin *efferre*, "to carry away." In such reading, attention is focused mainly on building the public meaning that is to be carried away from the reading: actions to be performed, information to be retained, conclusions to be drawn, solutions to be arrived at, analytic concepts to be applied, propositions to be tested. Such a stance usually dominates the reading of a textbook, a cooking recipe, a scientific report. The personal, sensuous, associative elements of consciousness are subordinated or ignored.

In contrast to the efferent focus of attention on what is to be retained *after* the reading, in the predominantly aesthetic stance, the reader focuses attention primarily on what is being lived through *during* the reading. The span of attention opens to attend not only to the public referents for the verbal symbols, but also to the sound and rhythm of the words in the inner ear and the sensations, images, associations, overtones, and memories that make up the qualitative state produced in consciousness by those words in that particular order. ("Aesthetic" is used to refer to attention to feeling, the qualitative, the experiential; whether a work of art emerges is a different, evaluative question.) When we read aesthetically, our attention is concentrated on what we are evoking from the page, on what we are seeing and feeling and thinking, on what is aroused within us by the very sound of the words, and of what they point to in the world of humankind and nature. The new experience we shape out of these elements, through a process of selection and synthesis, is for us the poem or story or play. Moreover, we respond to the very literary work that we are creating under guidance of the text (Rosenblatt, 1978).

Every reading act falls somewhere on the continuum between the efferent and the aesthetic poles. Most readings probably fall somewhere near the middle of the continuum; i.e., attention encompasses both public and private areas of consciousness that are resonating to the words, but in different proportions, according to the reader's purpose.

In predominantly efferent reading (for example, the reading of a book about ecology), the cumulation of information would be the predominant interest, but some associative, affective elements might be appropriately admitted into the range of attention. Similarly, in aesthetic reading, there is always an efferent, referential component, but attention centers mainly on the spectrum of feelings, sensations, associations, and ideas, in which the referential meanings are embedded.

Note that "efferent" and "aesthetic" refer to the reader's stance and not to the text. No matter what the intentions of the author or the linguistic potentialities of the text, any text can be read either efferently or aesthetically. A reader's purpose toward the same text may vary. The text of a poem, therefore, can be read efferently, if only its "literal" meaning is desired, or a novel can be analyzed efferently as a social document. And it is a cliché to speak of mathematicians who look at their solutions aesthetically and admire their "elegance." Unfortunately, there has been a failure to do justice to this aspect of the reading process.

The reader may clearly adopt one or the other, either the aesthetic or efferent, as the predominant stance. Much reading seems muddled or counterproductive at present because of the reader's confusion about stance. Thus, a political statement may be read with too much dominance given to the affective, associative elements, when the reader's purpose presumably is to discover verifiable reasons for, say, what taxation policies should be adopted. Much reading of advertisements fits that pattern. Even more pervasive is the efferent reading of stories, poems, and plays, with the consequent loss of their essential experiential qualities and values as works of art.

The fact that the text of a poem or a story may be read efferently—producing what often is referred to as its literal meaning—should not be interpreted as confirmation of the popular notion that the literary or aesthetic character of a work is a kind of ornamentation superimposed on the literal meaning—a view that I have termed the "jam on bread" theory of poetry. Aesthetic reading requires an integrated apprehension of the referential impregnated with all the qualitative, experiential constituents of the "sense" of words. Instead of thinking of the aesthetic as the literal plus the poetic, it might be more accurate to think of the referential as the aesthetic minus the personal, private aspects of meaning. However, both of these formulations fail to do justice to the reading act. We are not dealing with literal or affective, efferent or aesthetic, entities but with complex states of mind. Out of these, by a process of selection and under the guidance of the text, the reader carves structures of thought and feeling. Efferent reading involves objective referents plus attitudes and feelings; aesthetic reading involves emotion and thoughts about the world impregnated with affect. The difference lies in the proportions; the emphasis, dependent on the purpose of the reader.

Mature readers are able to adopt the stance that will enable them to carry out the selective and synthesizing process appropriate to their purposes. In most instances, the aim is to adopt the stance most appropriate to the text—to discover what the author may have intended. Often, this reflects the purpose which led the reader to that text—such as the search for information, the need for clarification of an issue, with the attendant adoption of the efferent stance. The desire for the pleasure, the experiences, the relaxation, and the insight, offered by novels, poems, or plays may lead to such a text, with the consequent adoption of the predominantly aesthetic stance. Sometimes an external cue, such as the description on a dustjacket, triggers the stance.

When the text is encountered without such prior selection of stance, the reader seeks cues within the text itself that signal which stance to adopt. Obvious cues of this sort are the wide margins and uneven lines that alert us to the possibility of evoking a poem. We may be invited to conjure up the characters and situations of a novel through such cues as the diction, the dialogue, the situations described, the narrative tense. Conventions such as the "once upon a time" opening, highly metaphoric expressions, verse forms, rhyme, or content such as fantasy may announce the need for the adoption of the stance.

In another context, it would be possible to translate the usual descriptions of critical reading into terms of the predominant stance. All reading transactions require careful elimination of irrelevant, projective, elements that are not supported by the text. The danger of excessive selectivity, of ignoring parts of the text, must be equally avoided. Efferent reading requires a stringent selectivity, an abstracting of the public meaning from its personal resonances, a testing of whether any attitudes or qualitative states aroused during the transaction are consonant with the efferent purpose.

The aesthetic stance requires keen attention to the inner reverberations of sound and sense, a readiness to hold in the memory the states of mind and the images evoked, and to build out of them an emergent structure that becomes the lived-through story or poem. Critical reading is a matter of critical attitudes toward the reader's personal contribution, as well as toward the structure of ideas or experience that is being created out of the transaction with the text.

The mature, skilled reader usually selects the appropriate stance automatically, as with other reading skills. But this act of selective attention must be learned by the child. Adults may give explicit indications as to stance or indirect suggestions, through the atmosphere surrounding the reading, through the reactions of adults to texts, through the kinds of expectations of performance implied in the questions habitually raised before and after readings. The false assumption that the text dictates the reader's stance has unfortunately resulted in concern with the question of what texts to present to students, with little or no help in differentiating the appropriate stance.

The Efferent Bias

An inordinate overemphasis on the efferent has been the consequence. Our technologically-oriented society, our mainly extrovert culture, has favored language in its public, impersonal, instrumental, scientific manifestations. This imbalance prevailed long before the current swing toward the narrowly practical and the scientific in our schools and universities and the decline in support of the arts. During the past half-century, the post-Sputnik pressure for scientific and technological advance has reinforced this aspect of our national ethos. Perhaps this partially explains why the teaching of reading in the schools has been based on models of the reading process that have not taken into account aesthetic reading. At best, the aesthetic (or literary) has been considered a variation on the efferent process requiring only the addition to it of new skills or strategies, not a different stance.

Preoccupation with different methods of inculcating the skills, essential though that is, has centered almost entirely on the cognitive, informative aspects of reading. Tests of reading comprehension reflect this bias toward the efferent. Basal reading texts and their teacher manuals manifest the same partiality. Stories and poems, introduced because of the young child's obvious interest, are nevertheless surrounded by the same kinds of questions as would apply to a purely informative text. The implication is clearly that stories and poems should be approached in the same way as such texts. I cannot resist citing again the poem in a third grade workbook headed with the question, "What facts does this poem teach you?" This question, in its call for an efferent stance even in the reading of a poem, epitomizes the general cumulative effect of most reading instruction, even when poems and stories are included. (Of course, once the aesthetic reading of that text had been honored, it might be entirely appropriate to discuss the new information received through the experience. But that is not why or how the poem should have been read in the first place.)

Even when, in later school years, the curriculum includes the "study of literature," the approach is often primarily efferent, with the accent on students' reporting their memory of details, and recounting the sequence of ideas or events. A similar approach prevails as students move into high school and college. Even when they achieve an aesthetic experience, they are often hurried away from it to efferent concerns, paraphrases, analyses, proofs that they have read the text and have understood it (efferently). Students are seldom encouraged to savor the experience, to linger on, recall or reenact the nuances, tones, and states of consciousness produced by the lived-through images, ideas, and events. Criticism should have such experience as its object.

Recent studies explicitly centered on children's entrance into the realm of literary or linguistic art are hampered by dependence on the (until recently) dominant formalistic literary theory, which identified literary art with product rather than process, and by traditional psychological methodology. Experimental designs purporting to deal with some element of art (e.g., metaphor) often seem rather to test the children's efferent, metalinguistic capacities, their ability to abstract or to categorize (Verbrugge, 1979). Since the literary and philosophical experts have shared the general preoccupation with efferent analysis, one cannot be astonished that psychological studies of art reveal the same bias.

The neglect of the aesthetic admittedly reflects unfortunate trends in our culture, and applies to all uses of language, spoken and written. The situation raises questions relating to mental health (Jones, 1968), and to fostering involvement of both hemispheres of the brain (Sagan, 1977). The importance of the affective and the imaginative in furthering cognitive growth is evidently only starting to be investigated (Ives & Pond, 1980; E. Saltz et al., 1979).

As late as 1968, Rommetveit, one of the few psychologists interested in "the capacity of words to encode and evoke affective states" (p. 141), pointed out that research in this area was fairly recent. The preoccupation with children's efferent use of language may have been reinforced by Piaget's studies of cognitive development. Bruner (1977) chose 1975 as the date to mark the beginning of "a new and interesting period...in which experience and function had emerged afresh as central to our understanding of what makes it possible for the child to pass so quickly, and so seemingly effortlessly, into the initial use of language." It is encouraging to note psychologists' increasing interest in the development of affect or emotion (Emde et al., 1976; Lewis & Rosenblum, 1978; Pliner et al., 1973). The problem of the development of awareness and expression of affect remains to be explored.

The Aesthetic as Basic

It does not seem too bold to hypothesize that in the earliest years, the capacity for the aesthetic mode of approaching experience may be primary. Children's prelinguistic and early language processes resemble or parallel the aesthetic stance. The following suggests the purposiveness of these processes, and reaffirms the importance of the inner organismic matrix in the early years.

> Beginning about the last quarter of the first year and continuing through the second, increased differentiations of self and other, the sharpening of self-awareness and the self-concept, and the ability to form and store memories enable the infant to begin the development of affective-cognitive structures, the linking or bonding of particular affects or patterns of affects with images and symbols, including words and ideas....
>
> Since there is essentially an infinite variety of emotion-symbol interactions, affective-cognitive structures are far and away the predominant motivational features in consciousness soon after the acquisition of language. (Izard, 1978, p. 404)

Poet Dylan Thomas told a friend, "When I experience anything, I experience it as a thing and as a word at the same time, both amazing" (Tedlock, 1963, p. 54). Doesn't this suggest a parallelism with the child's early "cognitive-affective structures," the child's seeing the word "cow" as an attribute along with its color, shape, or threatening bigness? (Bates, 1979, p. 60). Another trait related to the aesthetic stance is children's attention to and delight in the sound of words and recurrent rhymes and rhythms. Accounts of children's earliest responses to stories and poems read to them support this view of the interplay of experience and language, the "backward and forward flow between books and life" (White, 1954, p. 13).

Children's early receptivity to the aesthetic has been noted by parents and teachers, and is reflected in the constantly increasing publication of children's books and writings about them. Traditionally, children are offered verses, poems, and stories, and their playacting is encouraged. However, children's tastes for these are usually phrased as delight in the imaginative or fantasy. This is surely a powerful interest, and I should be the last to minimize its importance. Yet imagination is required for the real as well as the fictive, and my concern is with stance, which transcends or cuts across the distinction between the real and the make-believe. Emphasis on the text rather than stance has undoubtedly contributed to the tendency to equate the imaginative with the aesthetic. Not enough attention has been paid to the fact that stories about both the real and the make-believe are apprehended by the child with the same immediacy, the same linkage of word, object, and inner feeling that can be termed aesthetic.

The confusion of the aesthetic with the fictive, make-believe, may also underlie the belief that the child's early aesthetic predisposition is a passing phase. "With the start of school," we are told, "there is a subtle yet decisive shift in the child's explorations. An interest in stories and games continues. . . . But at the same time the child withdraws from the worlds of the imaginative and the fantastic, electing to remain securely surrounded by events and objects of the real world. . ." (Winner & Gardner, 1979; Chukovsky, 1963). One can understand that the child's problem of delimiting the objects and nature of the real

Rosenblatt

world may at a certain stage foster a preoccupation with clarifying the boundary between reality and fantasy. Yet, if literary art is equated with such elements as fictive content or metaphor, the reported distrust of fantasy may be confused with a rejection of aesthetic experience. The possibility of the aesthetic approach to texts presenting the real or the historic is overlooked.

This leads one to question to what extent rejection of fantasy is the product of the eagerness of home and school to precipitate efferent delimitations and to reward success in the efferent approach. How much of this loss of interest is due to education (Jones, 1968, p. 65)? The anthropologists remind us how alert young humans are to the subtlest signals that enable them to become assimilated to their cultural environment (Bateson & Mean, 1942; Benedict, 1934; Geertz, 1973). Surely, children are not insensitive to the fact that the greatest rewards come from demonstrating efferent understanding, that a poem or story is often to be read as a means of proving skills of efferent comprehension.

Of course, children need to conceptualize the real world; as adults they will need to handle abstractions. How can the referential, logical thinking of children be fostered without sacrifice of the rich organismic, personal, experiential basis of both efferent and aesthetic thinking? Isn't it our task to keep alive children's explorations of the world through seeing, hearing, touching, manipulating, and awareness of corresponding inner states? These are the roots of thought and language, both realistic and fantastic, aesthetic and efferent. Instead of accepting the notion of a remission of aesthetic sensibilities, we should make sure that our early reading programs do not permit them to wither away.

We are told that in adolescence children again become receptive to fantasy and the metaphorical (Winner & Gardner, 1979). Children's personal and interpersonal concerns at that stage provide a potential bridge into literary works. Some children, through fortunate home, school, and community influences, have retained their early capacity to respond aesthetically. But for most children, there has been an erosion of the habit of attention to inner states associated with the printed word. High school and college teachers sometimes resort to desperate strategies to interest students in literature, and especially to induce them to read poetry. An important impediment is the instructor's own persistence in promoting and rewarding formalistic efferent approaches. Aesthetic transactions with texts lead to personal involvement in the lived-through situations, characters, experiences. This is propitious to critical reflection both on the author's art that made them possible and on their significance for the readers' own lives (Rosenblatt, 1976).

Reading becomes no more than an empty skill, a rote exercise, if it does not relate to the needs, interests, and aspirations of the reader. Just as children develop language through their earliest efforts to understand and control the world and the self, so as readers (from the very beginning) they should be helped to feel that the transaction with the text has a meaningful personal purpose. The selection of a stance becomes a particular reflection or dimension of their broader life purposes. Such readers will acquire the capacity to appropriately handle personal responses to the printed word, and to manage critically the whole gamut, from the impersonal public knowledge of the scientist's text to the lyricism of the poet's.

Footnote
[1]The author's text also emerges from a personal and social transaction, but as the reader encounters only the text, we can deal simply with the reading act, through which communication takes place. Also, the interrelationship between writing and reading in the child's development cannot be treated here, but deserves full attention.

References
Auden, W.H. *Collected poetry*. New York: Random House, 1945.
Bateson, G. *Mind and nature*. New York: E.P. Dutton, 1979.
Bateson, G., & Mead, M. *Balinese character*. New York: New York Academy of Sciences, 1942.
Benedict, R. *Patterns of culture*. Boston: Houghton Mifflin, 1934.
Bruner, J., Caudill, E., & Ninio, A. Language and experience. In R.S. Peters (Ed.), *John Dewey reconsidered*. London: Routledge & Kegan Paul, 1977.
Chukovsky, K. *From two to five*, M. Morton (Trans.). Berkeley, California: University of California Press, 1957.

Deese, J. Cognitive structure and affect in language. In P. Pliner et al (Eds.), *Communication and affect*. New York: Academic Press, 1973.

Dewey, J. Qualitative thought. *Philosophy and civilization*. New York: Capricorn, 1963.

Dewey, J. The reflex arc concept in psychology. *Psychological Review* 1896, 3, 357-370 (Reprinted as The unit of behavior in *Philosophy and civilization*.)

Dewey, J., & Bentley, A.F. *Knowing and the known*. Boston: Beacon Press, 1949.

Drucker, J. The affective context and psychodynamics of first symbolization. In N.R. Smith and M.B. Franklin (Eds.), *Symbolic functioning in childhood*. New York: Halstead, 1979.

Emde, R.R., Gaensbauer, T.J., & Harmon, R.J. *Emotional expression in infancy*. New York: International Universities Press, 1976.

Gardner, H., & Wolf, D. (Eds.). *Early symbolization*. San Francisco: Jossey-Bass, 1979.

Geertz, C. *The interpretation of cultures*. New York: Basic Books, 1973.

Halliday, M.A.K. *Learning how to mean*. New York: Elsevier, 1975.

Halliday, M.A.K. *Language as social semiotic*. London: Edward Arnold, 1978.

Ives, W., & Pond, J. The arts and cognitive development. *High School Journal*, 1980, 63, 335-340.

Izard, C.E. *Human emotions*. New York: Plenum Press, 1977.

Izard, C.E. On the ontogenesis of emotions and emotion-cognition relationships in infancy. In M. Lewis and L.A. Rosenblum, *The development of affect*. New York: Plenum Press, 1978.

Lewis, M., & Rosenblum, L. *The development of affect*. New York: Plenum Press, 1978.

Ornstein, R.E. *The nature of human consciousness*. San Francisco: W.H. Freeman, 1973.

Pliner, P., Krames, L., & Alloway, T. *Communications and affect*. New York: Academic Press, 1973.

Rommetveit, R. *Words, meanings, and messages*. New York: Academic Press, 1968.

Rosenblatt, L.M. Toward a transactional theory of reading. *Journal of Reading Behavior*, 1969, 1, 31-47.

Rosenblatt, L.M. *The reader, the text, the poem*. Carbondale, Illinois: Southern Illinois University Press, 1978.

Sagan, C. *The dragons of eden*. New York: Random House, 1977.

Saltz, E., Dixon, D., & Johnson, J. Training disadvantaged preschoolers in various fantasy activities: Effects on cognitive functioning and impulse control. *Child Development*, 1977, 48, 367-380.

Tedlock, E. (Ed.). *Dylan Thomas*. New York: Mercury, 1963.

Verbrugge, R.R. The primacy of metaphor in development. In E. Winner and H. Gardner, *Fact, fiction, and fantasy in childhood*. San Francisco: Jossey-Bass, 1979.

Vygotsky, L.S. *Thought and language*. Cambridge, Massachusetts: MIT Press, 1962.

Weizsäcker, C.F. *The unity of nature*, F.J. Zucker (Trans.). New York: Farrar, Straus, & Giroux, 1980.

Werner, H., & Kaplan, B. *Symbol formation*. New York: Wiley, 1963.

White, D. *Books before five*. New York: Oxford University Press, 1954.

William, J.P. Learning to read: A review of theories and models. In F.B. Davis (Ed.), *The literature of research in reading*. New Brunswick, New Jersey: Rutgers Graduate School of Education, 1971.

Winner, E., & Gardner, H. *Fact, fiction, and fantasy in childhood*. San Francisco: Jossey-Bass, 1979.

Part Four
Schooling and Literacy

This section includes papers from three educators who look critically at school language practices in the light of current theory and research on the developmental relationships among language, thought, and literacy. Together they provide guidance for teachers who wish to adopt a new and fundamentally more solid view on which to base practices for assisting students' progress in all three areas.

Parker sets the tone for the section with a paper outlining the value of a theory of language and thought. He then applies the theory to an examination of the school's contribution to intellectual development as it can be seen in the results of a series of language interaction studies. Asking "If the growth of mind is sociocultural in origin, what kinds of growth are promoted or inhibited by schools?" Parker concludes that classrooms in England and America appear to involve students in verbal interactions that make the least direct and powerful contribution to their mental growth.

Parker then presents Barnes' suggestions (1970, 1975, 1977) for language use which might lead to increased levels of thinking, noting that these suggestions assume the transformation of interpersonal language processes into intrapersonal understandings and structures of thought.

Davis extends the interactionist-constructivist emphasis by suggesting that teachers' systematic observation and analysis of children's speaking, writing, and reading should form a basis for designing mediation strategies to guide and shape linguistic and intellectual growth. Such mediation, carefully distinguished from the typical intervention techniques imposed upon children, is characterized by its foundation on principles of developmental growth and it's considerations of context.

Through examples drawn from systems of functional analysis, Davis proposes several practical methods of mediation and concludes with the suggestion that all of us listen and attend more closely to children's expressive language.

Because he writes from an anthropological point of view, Smith's paper is the most distinctive of the three. He defines culture of literacy as the set of values, beliefs, techniques, skills, and social status associated with reading and writing. Stressing that our understanding of what constitutes reading and writing is dependent upon cultural factors, and has typically been a psychological view, he describes three traditional ways literacy is approached: from the standpoint of individual or group responses to reading and writing, from the perspective of their importance to people, and from the ways they are treated as a societal commodity.

The second half of Smith's paper draws implication for literacy teaching in schools from ethnographic studies of schools based on his concept of the culture of literacy. The promise held forth is that through our use of the concept we can gain new understandings of children and a heightened appreciation of community.

Schooling and the Growth of Mind*

Robert P. Parker
Rutgers University

Bruner's phrase "the growth of mind" serves two broad purposes in this paper. First, the word "mind" casts a wider conceptual net than cognition, which has the stark, technical flavor of many current psychological terms, or thought, whose meaning is too limited by everyday use. At the same time, mind is more directly useful in discussions of educational goals and practices than consciousness, which often evokes images of mind-altering chemicals or other suspect practices.

Nonetheless, I intend "mind" to encompass the various modes of knowing discussed in recent years by psychologists and philosophers, including serious researchers identified with the "consciousness movement." Mind makes possible an overarching definition of human consciousness, thus allowing me to consider knowing through action, imagery, and symbols (Bruner, 1973a, 1973b); knowing logically and sequentially or intuitively and holistically (Ornstein, 1972, 1976); knowing discursively or presentationally (Langer, 1942, 1973); knowing tacitly or explicitly (Polanyi, 1964, 1967); and knowing through feeling as a mode of intelligence (Witkin, 1976).

The word "growth" also is useful, pointing as it does toward a view of mind as both a living process and a life process. The growing mind is not an entity, not an achieved set of qualities or abilities; rather, it is a "set of processes which are always in motion and in change" (Cole & Scribner, 1975). Mind *is* its processes; therefore, it is always evolving, always forming and

---

*An earlier and shorter version of this paper was published in *CEA Critic*, 1982, 44.

never formed, always different now from what it was the previous moment, though what it is this moment, in use, is always the result of its developmental history of use.

Mind evolves from the unceasing transactions between the brain, in the course of its biological maturation, and the social and natural world. Through these unceasing transactions, brain becomes mind, and each society (and each culture) deeply and permanently influences this evolutionary course by the events it provides for its members.

In the United States, Mead (1934) first described the importance of society and social interaction in the development of mind. Mead claimed our thinking develops through our incorporation of the viewpoints of other people into our processes of thinking. Through our interactions with an increasing variety of others, we come to "know" their viewpoints and to take them into account in our own thinking. Eventually, we develop a sense of what Mead called the "generalized other," a conception of what others know and are thinking which guides us in adapting our mentation to social reality. The wider the range of viewpoints represented in our generalized other, the greater the growth of our mind.

At the same time, in Russia, Vygotsky was presenting a similar view of the fundamental roles society and culture play in the development of mind. Vygotsky chose as his starting point the dialectical materialism of Marx and Engels. From this base, he attempted to create a theory of mental development which took as its central fact the evolution of mind through a social-historical process, determined in its particulars by the specifics of the culture in which the development occurs.

Crucial to each culture are the kinds of productive activities it sponsors, including both manual and mental labor. Through their productive activities people alter both the course of their real existence and their thinking. Thought, and the products of thought, are shaped by the uses of thought in society. Thus, to understand the course of mental development, it is necessary to trace it from its origins in biological processes through its history of productive social activity, and the transformations thus produced, to the resulting higher psychological functions. Or conversely, to understand the evolution of higher psychological functions,

> we must arrive at a new concept of development itself. *Within* a general process of development, two qualitatively different lines of development, differing in origin, can be distinguished: the elementary processes, which are biological in origin, on the one hand, and the higher psychological functions, of sociocultural origin. (Vygotsky, 1978)

The history of mental development emerges from the interweaving of these two lines. The psychologist, hypothesizing that "behavior can only be understood as the history of behavior," faces the task of determining the important events, stages, transformations which constitute the history of that process and mapping their course.

More recently, Bruner presented a theory of mental development which, like Vygotsky's, emphasizes the role played by culture. Though his analysis is not undertaken from a Marxist point of view, Bruner argues that man's

> growth as an individual depends upon the history of his species—not upon a history reflected in genes and chromosomes but, rather, reflected in a culture external to man's tissue and wider in scope than is embodied in any one man's competence. Perforce, then, the growth of mind is always growth assisted from the outside...the limits of growth depend on how a culture assists the individual to use such intellectual potential as he may possess. (Bruner, 1973c, p. 52)

Central in this process of the growth of mind is humankinds' "development and use of tools or instruments or technologies that make it possible for him to express and amplify his powers." These instruments, which individuals make to amplify their powers of action, of the senses, and of the thought processes, are the products of their labor and, in turn, they alter their capacities for thinking. Through them, people may extend their consciousness into new realms, thus enabling them to produce further instruments and, eventually, further alterations of the nature of mind in that culture.

Bruner calls this view of mental development "evolutionary instrumentalism," and though his view lacks Vygotsky's explicit historical sense, it seems fair to include both his and Vygotsky's theories under this heading.

Beyond their general theories of mental development, and the role culture plays in the developmental process, both psychologists assign language a primary role in the growth of mind. As both a cultural product and an instrument of thought, language, once acquired, inexorably shapes the successive transformations of mental behavior which constitute the growth of mind. Vygotsky has the following to say about the function of language in the early years:

> The specifically human capacity for language enables children to provide for auxiliary tools in the solution of difficult tasks, to overcome impulsive action, to plan a solution to a problem prior to its execution, and to master their own behavior. Signs and words serve children first and foremost as a means of social contact with other people. The cognitive and communicative functions of language then become the basis of a new and superior form of activity in children. (Vygotsky, 1978, pp. 28-29)

So for Vygotsky, unlike Piaget, language initially serves a social function, and the cognitive and communicative functions evolve from this first general use. Labeling is one of the earliest cognitive functions.

Once children's use of speech for cognitive purposes is no longer limited to labeling,

> the intellectual mechanisms related to speech acquire a new function...a synthesizing function, which in turn is instrumental in achieving more complex forms of cognitive perception. (Vygotsky, 1978, p. 32)

Bruner's view of language, though similar, is not identical. For him,

> language is perhaps the ideal example of /a/ powerful technology, with its power not only for communication but for encoding reality, for representing matters remote as well as immediate, and for doing all these things according to rules that permit us both to represent reality and to transform it. (Bruner, 1973b, p. 470)

And further, at the far end of its continuum of uses for thinking:

> The important thing about language as an instrument of thought is not that one can translate actions or imagery into the new coin of words

and sentences. Rather, it is that the new medium allows one to transform what one has put into it into a new and powerful form that is not possible by other means. The productive rules of language, its combinatorial richness, is potentially available as a means for going beyond experience. In this sense it is the powerful tool for innovation. (Bruner, 1976, p. 74)

As a result of its syntax, its productive rules, its combinatorial richness, language serves as an instrument for the development of "analytic compentence":

the prolonged operation thought processes exclusively on linguistic representations, on propositional structures, accomanied by strategies of thought and problem-solving appropriate not to direct experience with objects and events but with ensembles of propositions. (Bruner, 1976, p. 72)

Analytic competence is concerned with possibility rather than reality, with all the relations theoretically possible among a set of propositions without reference to empirical reality. Only the particular grammatical structure of verbal language permits the development of analytic competence in thought as a transformation of communicative competence in speech.

Viewed through the lens of Bruner and Vygotsky's evolutionary instrumentalism, the growth of mind is seen as being sociocultural in its origins and historical in its developmental course. This historical course consists of "a complex interaction of the individual with the social context in which he exists." Language, as a product of culture and an instrument of thought, "plays a central and strategic role" in this history (Walkerdine & Sinka, 1978).

From this viewpoint, what might we hypothesize about important cultural institutions like schools? Schools are "language-saturated" institutions. What are their language policies and, through their language policies and practices, what role (or roles) do they play in the growth of mind?

Anthropologists and sociologists have increasingly focused their attention on schools as "distinct institutions of culture" (Brameld, 1963). They have come to see

the changing business of U.S. education as /a/ proper object of anthropological curiosity. That business consists of one particular institution demanding an ethnographic, or natural science, description and explanation of its own (Moore, 1976)

If schools, like other cultural institutions, play a part in the transmission and reproduction of culture (Bourdieu & Passeron, 1977), then it seems important to examine what we know of their language practices and of the possible effects of this aspect of enculturation on the growth of mind.

Despite wide differences in focus and methodology, and despite the small number of actual classrooms studied, the results of research undertaken to date on what Edwards and Furlong (1978) call "the language of teaching" reveal strikingly consistent patterns of verbal interaction across grades, subjects, and countries. The studies of spoken verbal interaction can be placed in three categories:

1. the studies initiated by Ned Flanders and his colleagues, plus subsequent studies using similar instrumentation;
2. the study of the language of selected secondary social studies undertaken by Arno Bellack and his associates; and
3. the analysis of teacher-pupil interchange across subjects in eleven first year secondary school classrooms by Douglas Barnes.

These studies represent a continuum from the selectively coded quantitative data produced for analysis by Flanders-type studies to the transcripts of full lessons analyzed qualitatively by Barnes.

Flanders and his colleagues sought to explain the "variations" which occur in chains of classroom events by keeping track of selected events which occur as part of these chains (Flanders, 1970). His method of investigation involved keeping a written record of those selected events on an observation form according to a coding scheme based on predetermined categories of events. Depending on their skill, the complexity of the categories, and the difficulty of the interaction being observed, observers trained in his coding scheme are able to record 10 to 30 symbols per minute. That is, up to 30 "events" per minute can be noted and categorized, though the average is usually closer to 20. Once the codings are complete, an analysis can be drawn, or a simple display can be created which shows how each event is part of the chain. Inferences about the chain of events can then be made. (Flanders, 1970)

These interaction analysis procedures focus only on selected features of the verbal communication in classrooms, ignoring all other events. Thus, they retain information about only part of one aspect of what constitutes the total chain of classroom events. Nonetheless, Flanders claims that the results obtained are rich enough and central enough to the educative process to be extremely helpful in a broader analysis of teaching behavior.

At the same time, Flanders describes the results of ten years of this "scattered and uncoordinated" research as discouraging. From kindergarten to graduate school, "teachers talk more than all the pupils combined," at an overall ratio of about two-thirds. In the classrooms studied, someone is talking about two-thirds of the time and teachers are talking about two-thirds of that time. The major problems, Flanders argues, are not ones of *quantity of talk*, but of *quality in talk*.

> *Item.* The percentage of all talk that appears as questions asked by the teacher can be estimated at: 13 to 16 percent in grades one through six (46), 10 to 12 percent in junior high school (38), and 6 to 8 percent in senior high school (74). These figures tell us little, but on the average, more than two-thirds of all teacher questions are concerned with narrow lines of interrogation which stimulate an expected response.
>
> *Item.* The percentage of all talk that appears as a teacher statement which reacts to or makes use of an idea previously expressed by a pupil can be estimated as 3 to 5 percent in grades one through six (46), 4 to 9 percent in junior high school (38), and 3½ to 8 percent in senior high school (74). This means that very little teacher talk is devoted to a consideration of ideas or opinions expressed by the pupils; their ideas are not dealt with adequately.
>
> *Item.* The percentage of all talk that appears as questions asked by the pupils varies with grade level, subject being studied, and so on, but the range is from about 1 percent to about 3 or 4 percent. It is shocking, however, to discover that less than 20 percent of these infrequently asked questions are thought-provoking questions; most pupil questions ask for clarification of directions or ask for statements to be repeated, etc.
>
> *Item.* When classroom interaction shifts toward more consideration of pupil ideas, more pupil initiation, and more flexible behavior on the part of the teacher, the present trend of research results would suggest

that the pupils will have more positive attitudes toward the teacher and the schoolwork, and measures of subject-matter learning adjusted for initial ability will be higher. A relatively small percentage increase in attending to pupil ideas, for example from 6 to 12 percent, has a constructive influence on educational outcomes. (1970)

Rosenshine (1971) discusses the results of these and other studies as they correlate with measures of pupil achievement, and notes that the findings are mixed. In the studies of classroom verbal interaction undertaken so far, he finds no patterns of teacher structuring statements, teacher questions, or teacher cognitive responses to pupil answers which show a consistent positive relationship to achievement as measured by standardized test scores. Despite this lack of clear patterns of relationship in the results, Rosenshine still concludes that "the frequency of teacher-pupil interactions concerned with intellectual growth significantly discriminated" between teachers of high and low achieving students.

To an extent, then, Rosenshine supports Flanders in his contention that the important problems which we can infer from patterns of verbal interaction between teachers and students are qualitative, not quantitative, as regards pupil achievement. At the same time, neither makes any claims about the possible relationships which might exist between these patterns of verbal interaction and their long-term influence on pupils' growth of mind.

Though considerably different in conception, focus, and methods, the Bellack et al. study (1966) of the language of 15 secondary social studies classrooms yielded results which, in some respects, complement and confirm the findings derived from Flanders-type interaction analysis. Bellack and his associates wanted, first, to describe the "patterned processes of verbal interaction that characterize classrooms in action." They hoped to determine who—teacher or pupil—"speaks about what; how much, when, under what conditions, and with what effect." Second, they were interested in looking at "linguistic variables of classroom discourse in relation to subsequent pupil learning."

Drawing from Wittgenstein, they viewed teacher-pupil verbal exchanges as "language games"; linguistic activities with definite structures and definite moves which participants engage in to achieve their purposes in particular settings. School language games, like all other language games, are rule-governed; to play them successfully, teachers and pupils must learn and follow the rules. From this viewpoint, they were able to isolate four "moves" typically made by teachers and students, to identify patterns among these moves, and to infer the rules governing the moves and their patterning. The moves were

> *Structuring.* Structuring moves serve the pedagogical function of setting the context for subsequent behavior by either launching or halting-excluding interaction between students and teachers.
>
> *Soliciting.* Moves in this category are designed to elicit a verbal response, to encourage persons addressed to attend to something, or to elicit a physical response. All questions are solicitations, as are commands, imperatives, and requests.
>
> *Responding.* These moves bear a reciprocal relationship to soliciting moves and occur only in relation to them. Their pedagogical function is to fulfill the expectation of soliciting moves; thus students' answers to teachers' questions are classified as responding moves.
>
> *Reacting.* These moves are occasioned by a structuring, soliciting, responding, or prior reacting move, but are not directly elicited by them. Pedagogically, these moves serve to modify (by clarifying, synthesizing, or expanding) and/or to rate (positively or negatively) what has been said previously. Reacting moves differ from responding moves; while a responding move is always directly elicited by a solicitation, preceding moves serve only as the occasion for reactions. Rating by a teacher of a student's response, for example, is designed as a reacting move.

Their findings for moves are reported as two sets of percentages: 1) the percentage of total moves represented by a particular move as initiated by teachers and pupils, and 2) the totals for particular teacher moves as percentages of their total moves and of the total lines spoken in the classrooms.

Tables 1 and 2 present the findings as they appeared in the original report. As Table 1 suggests, teachers in this study dominated three of the four moves: structuring, soliciting, and reacting. Their behavior left pupils with "a very limited role to play in classroom discussions." By and large, we can conclude these teachers set structures for discussions, initiated virtually all the exchanges, and evaluated both individual and group results.

Table 1

Pedagogical Move		1	Total	Percentage of Moves by Teachers	Percentage of Moves by Pupils	Percentage of Moves by Audio-visual Devices
Soliciting	SOL	5,135	100.	86.0	14.0	—
Responding	RES	4,385	100.	12.0	88.0	—
Structuring	STR	854	100.	86.0	12.0	2.0
Reacting	REA	4,649	100.	81.0	19.0	—

(p.46)

Table 2

Pedagogical Move		Percentage of Teachers' Moves	Percentage of Teachers' Lines
Soliciting	SOL	46.6	28.0
Responding	RES	5.5	6.8
Structuring	STR	7.7	20.1
Reacting	REA	39.2	44.7
Not Codable	NOC	1.0	0.4

f(Moves) = 9.565
f(Lines) = 30,897

(p.47)

Pupils did little other than respond to teachers' structuring/soliciting moves, and that little consisted mainly of rating other student responses when asked to do so by the teacher, soliciting information about work procedures, and structuring discussions when assigned to by the teacher. Pupils almost never spontaneously structured discussions, nor did they ever evaluate teachers' comments, spontaneously or otherwise. Teachers did make 12 percent of the total responding moves, but only 5.5 percent of the teachers' moves can be categorized as responding.

These figures on the proportional distribution of moves suggest an absence of dialogue between these social studies teachers and their pupils. If these teachers spent 54.3 percent of their talking time structuring and soliciting pupil response—in conducting monologues to set things up and get them going— then only 45.7 percent of their talking time was left for

Parker

interchange with students which might be called dialogue. If a further 5.5 percent of their talk was involved in responding to requests for procedural information and to other kinds of generally nonsubstantive requests, then only 40.2 percent of teacher talk—reacting—is left as potentially dialogic. When we consider that evaluations of pupil responses are included in the reacting category, then another major portion of teacher talk must be considered conversation ending rather than conversation extending. Certainly, as our own experiences in classrooms would suggest, the proportion of reacting talk that is evaluative must be at least half.

When Bellack and his colleagues analyzed the substance of these discussions, rather than the structure, they found other interesting results.

> By far the largest proportion of the discourse involved empirical meanings. This includes fact-stating and explaining, which accounted for between 50 and 60 percent of the total discourse in most classrooms studied. Analytic (defining and interpreting) and evaluative (opining and justifying) meanings were expressed much less frequently, each of them accounting for less than 10 percent of the discourse in any class. (p. 85)

Thus, whatever dialogue there might have been in these classrooms, whatever proportion of time might have been devoted to attending to pupils' ideas or to true interchange about course material, that time was mostly spent on stating and explaining matters of fact. Very little time, as Flanders also noted, was "devoted to a consideration of ideas or opinions expressed by pupils" (1970). In reality, as both groups of researchers have concluded, teachers spend very little time engaging students in such linguistic-intellectual activities as analyzing, synthesizing, speculating, hypothesizing, theorizing— what Vygotsky would call the "higher psychological functions" (1978). And if the growth of mind is "sociocultural in origin," then what kinds of growth are being promoted, or inhibited, by the patterns of language use in these classes? And if these classes are representative of classes in other schools and other subjects, then what must we hypothesize more broadly about the effects of schools, as a subculture, on the growth of mind?

Clearly, these are relevant questions to ask about the implicit language "policies" which these schools apparently have. However, before proposing answers to them, I want to look at two further status studies of school talk and one of school writing—all three undertaken in British secondary schools.

Two aspects of Barnes' pilot study (1971) bear directly on this discussion. First, Barnes broadly categorized all the questions teachers asked as either open or closed. Open questions invited more than one possible answer; closed questions clearly implied only one acceptable answer. Across the five subjects studied, open questions as a percent of the total questions asked ran from a low of 3.6 percent in Religious Education to a high of 48 percent in English; history was 23.5 percent. Because closed questions predominated (even in English) Barnes concluded that all the teachers were "teaching as though their tasks were more concerned with information than thought." Most of the time, these teachers

> were taking their task to be more a matter of handing over ready-made material, whether facts or processes, than a matter of encouraging pupils to participate actively and to bring their own thoughts and recollections into the conversation...pupils were seldom invited to think aloud, to generate new sequences of thought, to explore implications.

Barnes also found most of these teachers unaware of the gulf between their language, as subject specialists, and their pupils' nonspecialist language. As his analysis of the lessons revealed, the teachers' use of language frequently posed a barrier to pupils' learning.

> The teacher teaches within his frame of reference; the pupils learn in theirs, taking in his words, which "mean" something different to them, and struggling to incorporate this meaning into their own frames of reference. The language which is an essential instrument to him is a barrier to them. How can the teacher help his pupils to use this language as he does?

How can subject teachers help their pupils learn to think with the special language of the subject? How can pupils be helped to make this specialist language a part of their linguistic-conceptual apparatus? As Barnes observed, direct teaching of specialist terminology doesn't work. The many instances of that kind of teaching all seemed worthless, a waste of time. And answering closed-end questions calling for right answer production is not helpful either. Asking questions of the teacher, clarifying or exploring or evaluating others' responses, exchanging ideas back and forth openly: all of these activities by students would seem to lead to the growth in thinking which results from the incorporation of new viewpoints, new language, and new meanings into their existing linguistic-conceptual system. Yet, these are just the kinds of language activities these researchers found to be systematically excluded from classrooms by traditional teaching practices.

Not surprisingly, the picture for writing (Britton et al., 1975) approximates the one revealed for teacher-pupil talk. From ages 11-18, two dimensions of pupils' writing experiences narrow significantly. They do fewer kinds of writing for a narrower range of audiences. Their writing becomes more exclusively transactional in function (85 percent overall by age 18) and the audience becomes more and more "the teacher as examiner" (61 percent overall by age 18). Teachers are addressed less frequently as "trusted adults" or "partners in dialogue" and more often as the person concerned to see if right answers have been given or right forms produced.

This picture might appear less grim if the transactional writing done in later years required pupils to do increasingly higher order thinking—if it could be seen as contributing fully and powerfully to the growth of mind. Unfortunately, this was not found to be the case. Britton and his colleagues (1975) divided the informative wing of the transactional function into seven subcategories: record, report, generalized narrative, low level analogic, analogic, speculative, and tautologic. Like Moffet's spectrum of discourse, these categories represent an hierarchy of abstraction in thinking. Distressingly, only 4.1 percent of the total transactional writing, across subjects and years, is speculative or tautologic. That is, little of the writing involves either "the open-ended consideration of analogic possibilities" or "theory backed by logical argumentation." True, 14 percent of the writing done by 17-18 year olds fell into these two categories of writing that Vygotsky would likely say involved the "higher psychological functions," as opposed to 3 percent for 15-16 year olds, so there is some evidence of growth over the last two years of school. Nonetheless, 14 percent of the 17-18 year olds' writing is also in the report, generalized narrative, low level analogic categories. Seemingly, the writing assignments given the oldest students do not invite or require thinking that is much more complex than the assignments they had written on in earlier years. The students do not seem to have moved toward "analytic competence," at least not substantially. The teachers of these pupils on the whole do not see writing as a means to foster the "growth of mind," just as other teachers studied do not approach classroom talk as a means to intellectual development. Rather, they seem to remain concerned with pupils getting and reproducing information correctly without thinking about it or, and this is crucial, without using it to think with. Whether we call the most abstract mode of thinking analytic or tautologic, there is little evidence that teachers see this kind of thinking as a goal of their teaching. Or if they do, they must not see language as an instrument for achieving this goal.

Rosen comments in like vein on the Bellack findings. He notes that

> the teacher's carefully composed structuring and soliciting moves... have the disadvantage of tightly circumscribing the extent to which a pupil can formulate and represent in words what he is thinking. (Barnes et al., 1971)

To the extent that pupils' formulations of thought are circumscribed by the limitations placed upon the nature and quality of their dialogue, their thinking capacity is ultimately restricted.

> In dialogue, speakers take up statements that have gone before and develop them: one adds a qualifying condition, another suggests a cause or a result, another negates the whole statement, another reformulates it, and another qualifies one of the objects which it refers to...such a dialogue can be synthesized into a complex cognitive structure. Out of many such discussions comes the ability to think unsupported by the other participants in dialogue. (Barnes, 1977)

Thus, the *inter*personal processes of spoken and written dialogue are transformed into *intra*personal ones. Each operation incorporated into the growth of mind appears first, on the social (or interpsychological) level as an interaction among persons and second, on the individual (or intrapsychological) level as an inner thinking process. In Vygotsky's words: "All the higher functions originate as actual relations between human individuals" (1978).

This conception of the sociocultural origins of mind—or consciousness—highlights the role of dialogue, both spoken and written. If pupils have regular opportunities to engage in the kinds of dialogue, the "give and take of reciprocal discussions" (Barnes, 1976, 1977), which encourage and support higher order uses of consciousness, then the operations involved in these interactions may be reconstructed internally as permanent processes. When the opportunities for dialogue are sharply limited by the structure and content of classroom uses of language, then it would seem the growth of mind is sharply curtailed.

What may be the most telling fact about school language practices has not yet been mentioned. Almost nowhere in research on spoken interaction does there appear any evidence at all that schools support those modes of thinking and knowing variously called intuitive or presentational or tacit. In the Britton et al. research, poetic writing disappears almost entirely; by age 17-18 years it represents only 7 percent of the total writing done. This finding is paralleled by the results of other recent "writing across the curriculum" studies in the United States (Parker, 1981), Canada (McTeague et al., 1980; Fillion, 1979), and Australia (Bennett, 1978). The amount of poetic writing done by secondary school pupils across all subjects ranged from below 1 percent to just above 5 percent. Clearly, poetic writing is not valued, either for itself or for its contribution to intellectual development.

Yet, if our capacities for knowing, for consciousness and for the growth of mind are bimodal (as it seems likely they are), then the possibilities for development in one mode are virtually nonexistent while the possibilities in the other are severely restricted.

Perhaps teachers are not aware of this situation. Perhaps they do not know what they are doing, or not doing, in enacting these language practices and the policies they imply. I hope our obstruction of the growth of mind is unwitting, and that fresh evidence of the crucial role of dialogue in this process will lead us to formulate and enact new language practices and policies. The politics and economics of education, especially in this time of "back to basics," give little reason for optimism. Rather, I think current policies and practices will lead further toward what I can only conceive of as culturally transmitted mental retardation.

References
Amidon, E., & Hunter, E. *Improving teaching: The analysis of classroom verbal interaction*. New York: Holt, Rinehart and Winston, 1966.

Barnes, D. *From communication to curriculum*. Hammondsworth, Middlesex: Penguin, 1976.

Barnes, D. Language in the secondary classroom. *Language, the learner, and the school*. Hammondsworth, Middlesex: Penguin, 1971.

Barnes, D., & Todd, F. *Communication in small groups*. London: Routledge and Kegan Paul, 1977.

Bellack, A., et al. *The language of the classroom*. New York: Teachers College Press, 1966.

Bennett, B. The process of writing and the development of writing abilities 15-18. Paper presented at the Canadian Council of Teachers of English Annual Meeting, Ottawa, May 1979.

Bourdieu, P., & Passeron, J.C. *Reproduction in education, society, and culture*. London: Sage, 1977.

Brameld, T. The meeting of educational and anthropological theory. In G. Spindler (Ed.), *Education and culture*. New York: Holt, Rinehart and Winston, 1963.

Britton, J., et al. *The development of writing abilities 11-18*. London: Macmillan, 1975.

Bruner, J. Culture and cognition. *The relevance of education*. New York: W.W. Norton, 1973(a).

Bruner, J. Education as social invention. In G. Anglin (Ed.), *Beyond the information given*. New York: W.W. Norton, 1973(b).

Bruner, J. The course of cognitive growth. In J. Anglin (Ed.), *Beyond the information given*. New York: W.W. Norton, 1973(c).

Bruner, J. The growth of mind. *The relevance of education*. New York: W.W. Norton, 1973(d).

Bruner, J. Language as an instrument of thought. In A. Davies (Ed.), *Problems in language and learning*. London: Heinemann, 1976.

Cole, M., & Scribner, S. *Culture and thought: A psychological introduction*. New York: John Wiley, 1974.

Edwards, A.D., & Furlong, V.J. *The language of teaching*. London: Heinemann, 1978.

Fillion, B. Language across the curriculum. *McGill Journal of Education*, 1979, *14*.

Flanders, N. *Analyzing teaching behavior*. Reading, Massachusetts: Addison-Wesley, 1970.

Langer, S. *Mind: An essay on human feeling*, Vol. 1. Baltimore, Maryland: Johns Hopkins Press, 1973.

Langer, S. *Philosophy in a new key*. Cambridge, Massachusetts: Harvard University Press, 1942.

McTeague, F., et al. *An investigation of secondary student writing across the curriculum*. York, Ontario: Board of Education, 1980.

Mead, G.H. *Mind, self, and society*. Chicago: University of Chicago Press, 1934.

Moore, G.A. An anthropological view of urban education. In J. Roberts and S. Akinsaya (Eds.), *Educational patterns and cultural configurations*. New York: David McKay, 1976.

Ornstein, R. *The psychology of consciousness*. San Francisco: W.H. Freeman, 1972.

Ornstein, R. *The mind field*. New York: Grossman, 1976.

Parker, R. *Status survey of writing across the curriculum, phase I: A final report*. Mimeographed.

Polanyi, M. *Personal knowledge*. New York: Harper Torchbooks, 1962.

Polanyi, M. *The tacit dimension*. Garden City, New York: Doubleday Anchor, 1967.

Rosen, H. Toward a language policy across the curriculum. *Language, the learner, and the school*. Hammondsworth, Middlesex: Penguin, 1971.

Rosenshine, B. Teaching behavior related to pupil achievement: A review of research. In S. Westbury and A. Bellack (Eds.), *Research into classroom processes*. New York: Teachers College Press, 1971.

Vygotsky, L. *Mind in society*. M. Cole, S. Scribner, E. Souberman, and V. John-Steiner (Eds.). Cambridge, Massachusetts: Harvard University Press, 1978.

Vygotsky, L. *Thought and language*. Cambridge, Massachusetts: MIT Press, 1962.

Walkerdine, V., & Sinha, C. The internal triangle: Language, reasoning, and the social context. In I. Markova (Ed.), *The social context of language*. New York: John Wiley and Sons, 1978.

Witkin, R. *The intelligence of feeling*. London: Heinemann Books, 1976.

Developing Literacy:
Observation, Analysis, and Mediation in Schools

Frances A. Davis
Beaver College

Children's acquisition of the processes of speaking and writing during early childhood years warrants our attention. As components of their developing representational system, these processes and their products reflect children's underlying cognitive abilities and their social and emotional growth. Further, because language and thought are interacting systems, such representations function as a catalyst for intellectual growth.

Teachers can use a three-step process to focus attention on the ways children speak, write, read, and listen: 1) observation, 2) analysis, and 3) sensitive mediation. Observation of language interaction results in field notes which, in turn, become the material for analysis. The analysis, grounded in context, enables individual children's intentions in the use of language to be identified. In addition, the degree to which such intentions are fulfilled can be seen. Study of the analysis will yield a profile of children's patterns of language use and can provide a basis for developing teaching-learning mediation strategies to help children extend the range of their talk and writing.

The guiding or mediating way of shaping children's language forms contrasts with a behavioristic, skill-oriented, method. Mediating efforts are those activities which help children make more appropriate references and interpretations in the four language modes. As Ecroyd (1978) defines these processes, they are the ways children learn to make wise choices about the best way to communicate their thoughts.

In this paper, I suggest some ways we can observe and analyze children's language as well as some ways to develop mediation strategies. It is hoped the examples of several levels of observation and analysis and descriptions of programs using some of the suggested mediation techniques can aid teachers in finding additional ways to work with children. Beyond this, it is hoped that teachers who attempt thoughtful observation and analysis will be rewarded with increased insight into ways language functions for young children.

Observation

Before any useful action can be taken in relation to children's use of language, we first need to know what they can do with the language they have. Toward this end we can use checksheets, categorical notes, or anecdotal records to chart children's language use. These will include recordings in all of the language modes; however, depending upon our focus, one or another likely will receive emphasis. Often, because our desire is to know how children express their intentions in speech and writing, our notes will reflect these language efforts.

Observations of speech in early childhood classrooms is often difficult. Particular skill is needed to catch segments of dialogue because of the temporal nature of speech and children's frequently nonstandard articulations. In addition, extraneous noises often interfere. Providing the noise level is minimal, some speech sequences may be audiotaped. Most teachers, however, find it more practical to make shorthand notes. Kept as unobtrusive as possible, this method is especially valuable for noting interesting or spontaneous utterances. Regardless of method, we should keep in mind that it is unrealistic to try to record all important bits of talk. Some way of being selective in our observations needs to be found.

A sense of direction for selecting observation events can come from our purpose. If we wish to identify the limits of children's language use, we will look toward analyses which show us patterns in the way young children use language. Sometimes these recordings will be of a social nature; other times, our notes will reveal the children's intellectual processes or emotional states. Usually, our interest will focus on the extremes found in the children's language: divergent-language, shyness, hesitancy in speech, or communicative excellence. That is, in speech and writing, we will most likely look for examples of language limitations and examples of competence and creativity. An appraisal of these samples will help us develop mediation opportunities for expansion into new areas for highly competent children. Illustrations follow of some types of language uses we may encounter.

A Child with Divergent Language

Four year old Shirley Jane's story suggests how a language-divergent background leads to temporary limitation. A Japanese-American child, Shirley came to America on a ship with her parents and her 18 month old brother Jimmy. Her mother, devastated by sea sickness, left Jimmy in the care of his father. Unaccustomed to caring for a toddler, Shirley's father devoted most of his attention to Jimmy and left Shirley alone to wander around the ship.

This was Shirley's first immersion into a totally English language environment; she spoke little English prior to the voyage despite the fact that her father was an American. During the trip, however, she learned three basic words: "Shirley Jane wants. . . ." This phrase, with a bit of body language conveyed her meaning. At this point, she was a 4 year old child with a 2 year old's English vocabulary. Her range of communicative competence was narrowed as a result of cultural change.

However, Shirley quickly picked up new English vocabulary and syntax. Because of her young age and the responsiveness of the environment into which she was placed, she experienced little difficulty. Had she been older or in a different environment, the result might have been an unhappy one for her.

Inappropriate Language Use

Another 4 year old, Jeannie, provides an illustration of inappropriate and limited language use. Jeannie's teachers in the nursery school initially wondered if she might be retarded. She spoke little and usually wandered about aimlessly or played alone. The teachers felt she had not made the transition from solitary play to more social interaction with other children which usually occurs between ages 3 and 4. Concerned about her passive behavior and lack of verbalization, they requested an outside observer to make a series of observations.

Notes of Jeannie's behavior in the nursery school classroom revealed that she frequently tried to initiate conversations or join groups of children but that most of her efforts met rebuff. In addition, observations of her language interactions with her father during a father-child pancake breakfast indicated that she was capable of producing unusually mature language patterns. Following these early language and behavior notes, attention to Jeannie's use of language in the classroom revealed that her maturity put her at a social disadvantage with her peers. As a result, her speech timing was poor. She felt different from other children and hesitated to step into their conversations. A cycle developed: Jeannie hesitated and the other children, sensing her strangeness, began to exclude her from play activities. Invariably, her approach to a group would occur just as it was about to disband. Her slowness to join children in social play delayed her entrance to a group until it was nearly ready to break up or until all roles were assigned and there was no place left for her.

The observation and analysis of Jeannie's classroom behavior were helpful; her teachers set aside their concern about her intellectual ability and focused their attention on her language and social problems. Fortunately, they were able to mediate more productive encounters for her with other children by making use of her interest in rhythm and music. These activities helped her develop confidence, and she began to time her approach to other children more effectively.

For Jeannie, an outside observer made the notes of her behavior because the teachers felt they were too close to the situation to see it clearly. The observations that were made, however, could be made by teachers as they go about their routines. Staff room dialogue about the observations can aid in analysis and interpretation.

Creative Language Use

Both Jeannie and Shirley Jane used language in ineffective or limited ways with others. At the other end of the language use continuum was 3 year old Laura Elisabeth. Bright and effervescent, making up and telling stories was one of her special delights. She usually found a ready audience for her tales in some member of her family. Before she could write, she busily "wrote" many letters, lists, and stories. A series of these stories had a major character, King Dom Com. You can guess how she might have developed this name—the King that had a kingdom was King Dom Com. From this start, she developed articulate stories which followed the traditional story structure. Laura's creativity was fostered in the home by parents who were genuinely interested in literature and included reading as an everyday event. In addition, her modified Montessori school made special attempts to guide her language use into productive ways in various social situations.

The divergent-language child, the silent and shy, and the child who uses language in creative ways are all operating at different levels. Discerning these differences requires us to pay attention, to observe, and to analyze children's talking and writing. Analysis of the language samples can then reveal the ideas children hold and patterns of their language and behavior.

Analysis

The purpose set for observation determines the kind of analysis that will be undertaken. If speech is unclear and articulation a problem, we will give careful attention to speech sounds. If choice of words or sentence structure seems to cause limitations, the focus can be on these. For all children, there is relevance in a focus on the way they seem to be limited in language use and on the way they use language in competent ways to come to term with people, objects, and events in their lives. This focus can be achieved through two approaches: 1) From the samples collected, we can derive categories of use or 2) categories can be decided upon ahead of time and we can assign codes to each. Both methods have advantages and disadvantages. Finding categories within our samples can be time consuming. Yet, it may give us a more complete picture of children's use of language within context. Deciding ahead of time on particular categories has the advantage of allowing us to concentrate on those specific functions. We can then discern more quickly how effectively children use language in the areas selected.

Analysis Using Functional Categories

At the conference on Young Children's Use of Language held at Rutgers University, Joan Tough described the Communication in Early Childhood Project (Leeds University, England). Over 3,000 British teachers joined with their project team to collect children's language samples for analysis. The categories they used for this analysis were derived originally from categories of child speech analyzed by Tough during earlier research. These were the language uses of: 1) self-maintaining; 2) directing; 3) reporting; and 4) abstract uses labeled "toward logical reasoning" —projecting, predicting, and imagining. The following presentation of the system does not do it justice; however, it is helpful for us to understand what the categories entail. Tough defines these as:

1. *Self-maintaining.* A reference to a psychological or physical need, such as, "I want my milk." Or a projection of self-interest, as, "That's mine...that's my car, you can't have it, that's my car."
2. *Directing.* A self-reference, such as, "And now I put the red dot here, and I put the blue dot here, and then I move the cars along the dots." Or an effort to direct others, such as, "Now, I'll be the Mommy, and you be the little girl, and you be the Father, and you go out to

work and I will do the shopping." Such language sets the stage and plans the activities of surrounding children.

3. *Reporting.* A reference to past or present experience. Such an instance was observed recently during a "show and tell" session in a local nursery school. Responding to a friend's showing of a ceramic lamb, Johnny connected it to his own life. He said, "Oh, my mommie has a lamb just like that, only the head screws off and there's a bottle inside." He responded to a clue in the present time frame (the lamb) and verbally placed it in his past (his lamb at home). His reference connected a present, ongoing event, to a point in his life outside the present time frame.

4. *Toward logical reasoning.* Linguistic evidence of the use of logical operations such as classifying, seriating, predicting, justifying, explaining, or comparing. In the example of Stephen's fishing story (which follows), he says, "Wate fishing you catch big ones and not many...float fishing you catch small ones and lots of them." This comparison would fall in the logical reasoning category.

The ease with which most children's language fits these categories makes this system useful for teachers. There are, however, other systems of language functions which might be used to examine children's talk and writing. Two of the most comprehensive of these were developed by Halliday (1975) and Britton et al. (1971, 1975). The Halliday system is more extensive than is needed for most classroom use, though a study of the system would be valuable for increased understanding of language functions. The Britton functions—expressive, transactional, and poetic—lack the specificity most classroom instances require (Wight, 1977). It is true, however, that the elaboration of the Britton scheme, as developed in the writing abilities project of 11 to 18 year olds (1975), broke the transactional area into subcategories: Record, Report, Generalized Narrative, Low Level Analogic, Analogic, Speculative, and Tautologic. These are analogous to the categories outlined by Tough in that there is movement from lower to higher levels of abstraction. For teachers of young children, it would seem as Wight (1977) suggests that the Tough categories are more useful.

Focus on Cognitive Indicators

Indicators can be found in children's speech and writing which show us what cognitive operations underlie their use of such functions as identify, explanation, justification, and prediction. Information gathered about children in this way can aid us in knowing what kinds of thinking skills children are using and in what situations these are exhibited (Odell, 1977). Understanding these will suggest ways in which teachers can support the children's continued intellectual development.

Analysis of children's language for the purpose of identifying cognitive operations might follow the lines of one developed in a study of the storytelling of sixty 7 and 10 year old British children (Davis, in progress). In this study, each child told an original story and then wrote the same story for the investigator. The system for analyzing these stories was based on categories derived from the stories themselves. These included a tally of time and sequence relationships; distancing from self; audience awareness; relationship units of character, event, and setting; units of descriptive and positional reference; and logical thinking processes. The logical thinking category included such processes as explanations, comparisons, concessions, justifications, judgments, predictions, and deductions.

One story obtained from a child in this study illustrates the kind of analysis undertaken. In this story, Tony, a friend of Stephen, told about his fishing expedition. On the left side of the page is a copy of the story as Tony told it on tape; on the right side, his written version with the retention of original spelling and punctuation.

ORAL	WRITTEN
1. One day me an my friend Stephen were	One day I was going to go with my
2. going to go fishing in the summer	friend Steaphan fishing
3. It was summer holiday so we didn't have any days off school.	we got up at 6 o clock
4. His mom and dad were going to pick us	
5. up	
6. And we went on the train	We were going on the 7 o clock train
7. And when we got there we paid our	when we got there we Payed our
8. entrance fee to the ponds	entrance fee
9. And we went to a place that Stephen	And went in.
10. knew because Stephen often	
11. went fishing	
12. We got our lines out	We undid our acurpment
13. And we baited them	
14. And we threw them in	and carst out lines
15. Stephen's was weight fishing	We were there about 10 minits when
16. Stephen goes for big fish out in	I cawt a little tidaler
17. the deep end which you can only	In time we were having dinner
18. catch with weights	by that time I had cawt 8
19. I go for the little fish near the	and steaphan had cawt two.
20. sides which you can only get	he had only cawt two because he
21. with floats	was wate fishing
22. And after a little while Stephan	and I was float fishing
23. caught quite a big one	Wate fishing you catch big ones
24. And I caught a few tidley ones	and not many
25. as well	float fishing you catch small
26. (We call the little fish tidleys)	ones and lots of them.
27. One of my tidleys got away	
28. The next day we caught another big one	
29. And by the time his mom and	By the end of the day he had cawt 5
30. dad came to pick us up, we had	and I had cawt 37
31. caught quite a few	
32. We put them all back in	
33. (And Stephen) And near the end	
34. Stephen caught a really big one.	He had cawt one very big one
35. And he took it home	He bort that one
36. And he et that one.	His mom and dad came to pick us up
37. He had that one.	
38. His mother prepared it	
39. And they had it for tea.	When we went home we had it for tea
40. They had it with mashed potato.	

Davis

Tony matched his written story quite closely to the oral version. The same plot sequence carried over from the telling to the writing. He retained his ideas, made the same comparisons and explanations, and drew the same conclusions in both. However, the written story was more succinct than the oral version. This demonstrates important contrasts between the two processes of writing and talking. When telling the story, Tony did well without being able to review. Only once did he forge ahead and need to backtrack (at line 33). He also mixed up the time line (line 28) and confused the audience. In the writing, backing up was unnecessary as he was able to review his work and avoid the confusion. He also was more conscious of the audience in the oral version than in the written. He explained (line 26), "We call the little fish tidleys," an acknowledgement of the need for listener clarification. In the writing, Tony also had a chance to be more specific; he even included the number of fish caught.

Tony placed this story in the context of his own life—his desires and wishes for the future. Revealing an interest and knowledge about fishing, he shared it with his audience. His awareness was made clear in the oral version by the direct reference to the listener. This reference was not present in the written version. Perhaps this lack was an indication of Tony's sense that the written mode requires the author to assume a role at a greater distance from the reader. One might refer to this as the "etched in stone" sense that there is a certain formality which needs to be assumed when putting words on paper.

The analysis used for the study noted Tony identified character, event, and setting units (Tony and Stephen fishing in the pond). In the reference to Stephen as "my friend," he used a descriptive unit. Other descriptive units revealed the relationship of mom and dad, the kind of holiday it was, and the type of fishing each boy did. The sequence of events moved forward from paying fees for fishing to the next day...to "had it for tea."

"Stephen goes for the big ones because he uses weights and I go for the little tidleys and I don't use weights," inferred the logical thinking category. When he said, "He goes for the big fish with the weights and I go for the little fish," he compared, explained, and then concluded, "And we had it for tea, and they had it with mashed potatoes." Explanation also was present in, "It was summer holiday so we didn't have any days off school," and "We went to a place Stephen knew because Stephen often went fishing."

What does this kind of an analysis tell us about Tony's language development? Identifying the language functions he uses helps us know how Tony is using language in one setting. This evidence, together with other things known about his speech in everyday dialogue or school writings, helps build a profile of Tony's expressive use of language. Multiple observations would make up the profile and could aid Tony's teachers to develop realistic expectations about his contribution to discussions and other classroom work. Knowing Tony shows the ability to use language in ways which express logical thinking can be turned into instructional terms. Logical expression can, therefore, be required of him at other (but, not all) times. He can be expected to explain, justify action, and make comparisons. Extending these skills in other language situations, such as predicting science experiment results, would be appropriate school activities for him.

The writing Tony did in this storytelling session also indicated spelling forms similar to those found by Read (1976) and Clay (1975) in their studies of early writing. His consistency in phonetic spelling perhaps could be guided to more common forms within the context of his writing. Other conventions, capital letters, and completed sentences gradually could be brought to his attention.

Mediation

Accurate knowledge of the current functional levels of children's language use, through observing and analyzing their speech, and writing processes, is necessary for teachers who wish to help children grow toward increased language facility. Children's language, carefully noted and analyzed, will give teachers a basis for knowing what "next steps" might be taken. Through knowing the kinds of things children do with speech and writing, more accuracy can be made in stretching that language use to more advanced levels.

The focus of mediation strategies is on encouraging children to find additional means of expression. The goal is to help children extend their own language limits by being able to make sensible choices about the best ways to communicate meanings. Implied in this goal is the idea that children's intent is primary. We should encourage children to articulate their *own* meanings, not change or provide new meanings for them. Given the nature of language and its relation to cognition as we understand it from Piaget (1965) and Vygotsky (1962), we can expect new meanings may emerge in the children's talk and writing. These changes occur at the original source; they are not imposed upon children by an outside force.

Any list of mediating strategies would be endless. There are, however, some basic principles which apply to any mediation we might attempt with young children. Among these are the developmental expectation of egocentricity, the activity orientation of young children, and the developmental trend from concrete thinking to the more abstract.

From Piaget's research we have learned that the young child does not take events into consideration from another's perspective. That is, their perception is egocentric. This means that we will not expect young children ordinarily to consider the audience for which they write or talk. Further, it is important for us to understand that children construct their understandings in the context of their own activity. That context should be included in the appraisals we make. The normal path of intellectual growth from the concrete to the more abstract, from the figurative to the operative aspects of cognition, also should be taken into account. That is, young children move in the here and now time frame; therefore, they learn more easily when they can manipulate objects rather than use more abstract symbols which stand for the object.

The developmental principles mentioned above help us to know that children's language is concrete and context-bound. While drills within a specific setting may be helpful, they are of questionable value outside that setting. If children are given drills out of context or are constantly asked to provide unnatural utterances, such as complete sentences in casual dialogue, they can be expected to respond to teachers for psychological reasons unrelated to learning. Such responses make it difficult for children to generalize to other knowledge systems.

Removing skill acquisition from ongoing context also draws children's attention to the concrete activity of filling a page with marks of some sort. This does not help to move language into an abstract verbal system, and transfer of learning to other situations becomes minimal under such circumstances. This argument lies behind my earlier suggestions for helping Tony with the conventions of written language within the context of his own writing.

Keeping in mind the psychological stance of egocentricity, the need young children have for active, concrete, learning within context should guide the selection of direct and indirect mediation strategies. Additionally, basing strategies on observation and analysis of child speech and writing should increase our chances of helping children internalize learnings. Based on these developmental principles, the following three categories of suggestions are made: The use of explicit directions in contrast to inferred instruction, the use of dialogues to encourage thought development, and the construction of materials and activities for use in context.

Explicit Directions

Gumperz (1981) suggested that schools need to provide children with explicit direction rather than expecting them to infer the teacher's meaning. We do need to convey what we mean and not send the children hidden messages. One such hidden message frequently was sent by a nursery school teacher who said, "Tables are not for sitting," in an effort to help the small children learn school social rules. "Sit in the chair, John," would be more direct with the addition of, "We need to use the table for our games." This second form is more explicit and would satisfy two principles: Teachers would say what they really meant, and would provide a model of explanatory language for the children.

In order for teachers to become more direct and explicit in their instructions, they must be able to monitor their own talk. Tough (1979) emphasizes the importance of such monitoring by saying that teachers' talk must be selected with the same awareness and deliberation as is used in the selection of any other resource. When teachers do control their talk, it becomes a positive force toward learning. Such control includes the kinds of explicit and explanatory comments suggested previously and the avoidance of global or missing pronominal reference. We should also become more aware of the speech mannerisms we all have. For example, teachers who continually leave sentences unfinished provide poor models for children.

Dialogue Techniques

Strategies built on the observations and analyses undertaken by the teachers in the Tough project used dialogue to encourage thought development. Five strategies developed by this project could be useful for teachers in any setting. These were:

1. Orienting and inviting children to talk about ongoing events or explain a phenomenon occurring at the time;
2. Enabling, stimulating the child to give a full response to the teacher's request for information by asking for more detailed explanation or justification, or by using a focusing or checking strategy;
3. Informing, adding new information to that provided by the child;
4. Sustaining, encouraging added dialogue participation by using verbal or nonverbal means; and
5. Concluding, anticipating the ending of the dialogue in such a way as to complete it without leaving the child with the impression that the teacher had lost interest in what was being said.

The strategies outlined from the Tough project are techniques which can help us ask "open-ended" or creative-answer questions rather than "closed" questions—those questions which require one word or merely gesture responses. The goals of open questions are to solicit inferences, comparison-making, or other cognitive action. The use of the strategies gives us a guide to words which will help us move into open-ended questioning rather than simply directing us to change our questioning focus.

Materials and Activities Used in Context

Beyond dialogue and questioning interactions with children, teachers can use materials and activities in many mediating ways. For example, an understanding of classificatory systems has a better chance of becoming internalized when children handle objects and talk about their various attributes (Sigel, 1970). Likewise, the meaning of positional words can be fostered by using action games. Positional exercises (Stand in front, behind, or beside your chair; Susie is sitting behind Eric, stand in front of him now; Susie, pick up the crayon under the table, put it on top of the table, to the right, to the left, in the middle of the table) are ways one teacher used to accomplish this in a concrete and active manner. A more abstract level of this activity was an audiotape requesting children to position papers in front of them on the table in a particular way. The tape then continued with directions for the children to make drawings that were familiar to them: geometric figures in particular positons (in the middle, at the top left, and so on). When children finished the directional part of the activity, they checked their papers against a prepared model. The tape then moved them toward a more creative activity by instructing them to complete the picture in any way they liked as long as it was their own idea and not a copy of someone else's design or picture.

The teacher that used this audiotape activity designed it to help her 5 year old children learn to follow verbal directions, internalize geometric shapes, and learn the meanings of positional words. It could be used with a group of children; or as children increase in independence, it could become a solitary activity. In either case, the tape followed the physical, concrete, exercises. The children enjoyed working with the taped messages for the independence and control they were able to achieve. Further, each child's creative ending was acknowledged and valued; the "game" became a pleasant way of learning.

Aside from the control values of such activities as those described, the children gained practice and familiarity with language connected to classificatory and positional concepts. The fact that language aids conceptual understanding through its interaction with intelligence is stressed by psychologists who propose a constructivist point of view. Sinclair (1975), through her conservation experiments, showed that children who consistently used descriptive words along one dimension (short-long in contrast to little-long) showed greater understanding of the transformation. In a study of representational development, further substantiation was found for this connection. The manner in which children classified and labeled objects was closely correlated with their language abilities in storytelling and other graphic representation (Davis, 1975).

The strategies suggested in this paper urge us to base mediation on observation and analysis, to begin with young children where they are—in a concrete mode—and move toward greater abstraction. Some specific techniques suggested were: Building on developmental characteristics of the young child—noting egocentricism and propensity for action; using explicit rather than implicit directives; developing dialogues which call for inference and thought; and creating activities and materials within the contextual setting which help children connect language to conceptual understandings.

In addition to all of these suggestions, we need to tune into children's language by listening more attentively to them. We must increase our attempts to hear the difficult-to-understand child. The child with a speech impediment or hesitant speech needs to be heard and to receive responses from us. A part of this is the necessity for us to assert our rights for children and ourselves for an atmosphere where individual voices can be heard and attention gained and held. The impinging stimuli, competition for teachers' attention, and the noise found in many early childhood settings are detrimental to us all. A balance among freedom, openness, and creativity and an atmosphere for dialogue needs to be secured. All children need attentive listeners who model attending behavior and respond in meaningful ways.

References

Britton, J., et al. *The development of writing abilities 11-18*. London: Macmillan, 1975.

Britton, J. What's the use? A schematic account of language functions. *Educational Review*, 1971, *23*.

Davis, F.A. Linguistic and graphic representations, mental imagery and their relationship to cognitive levels in children aged three, five, and seven years. Unpublished doctoral dissertation, Rutgers Graduate School of Education, 1975.

Davis, F.A. Preparation for literacy: Holding one's own in narrative. In progress.

Ecroyd, D. Teaching for communication competence. In F.A. Davis and R. Parker (Eds.), *Teaching for literacy: Reflections on the Bullock Report*. London: Ward Lock, 1978.

Gumperz, J. Remarks made at the conference on enthography and education, University of Pennsylvania, 1980.

Halliday, M.A.K. *Learning how to mean: Explorations in the development of language*. London: Edward Arnold, 1975.

Odell, L. Measuring changes in intellectual processes as one dimension of growth in writing. In C. Cooper and L. Odell (Eds.), *Evaluating writing*. Urbana, Illinois: National Council of Teachers of English, 1977.

Piaget, J., & Inhelder, B. *The psychology of the child*. New York: Basic Books, 1969.

Read, C. *Children's categorization of speech sounds in English*. Urbana, Illinois: National Council of Teachers of English, 1976.

Sigel, I.S. The distancing hypothesis: A causal hypothesis for the acquisition of representational thought. In M.R. Jones (Ed.), *The effects of early experience*. Miami, Florida: The University of Miami Press, 1970.

Sinclair, H. The role of cognitive structures in language acquisition. *Foundations of language development*, Vol. 1. New York: Academic Press, 1975.

Tough, J. *Talk for teaching and learning*. London: Ward Lock, 1979.

Vygotsky, L. *Thought and language*. Cambridge, Massachusetts: MIT Press, 1962.

Wight, J. Speech acts: Thought Acts. *Educational Review Special Issues, Developments in Language*, 1977, *28*.

Reading and Writing in the Real World: Explorations into the Culture of Literacy

David M. Smith
University of Pennsylvania

Introduction

Rather than looking at reading and writing primarily as cognitive processes, or as skills with sociocultural dimensions, it is fruitful to view them as fundamentally sociocultural phenomena. While the two approaches may not necessarily be contradictory, until fairly recently, the latter perspective has not been characteristic of most research or practice in American education. This view underlies several recent studies of classroom interaction and of literacy in homes and communities. (Hymes et al., 1978-1979 in West Philadelphia; Smith et al., ongoing in Philadelphia; Heath, 5 year ethnographic study in the Southeastern United States; Liechter, et al., 1980-1981 in New York).

At the outset, this approach mandates a definition of "the real world" different from what would be expected. As used here, this phrase does not refer only to literacy activities which are confined to out-of-school contexts. The social context, school or otherwise, is not simply a setting to display a set of cognitive skills and knowledge which remains constant across settings, but is a key ingredient in the literacy event itself. So central is context to understanding literacy that it is easy to find that what counts as reading in one context will not count in others. Therefore, I take reading and writing in the real world to refer to the meanings of literacy in the cultural contexts in which individuals or groups live their lives.

173

Whereas cognition has become a central and analytic construct in traditional school-centric views of literacy, understanding reading and writing in the real world requires an examination of the culture of literacy. Though this notion, which becomes our primary construct in the present discussion, is defined more precisely as the discussion progresses, a simple definition is in order at this point.

The culture of literacy refers to the values, beliefs, techniques, skills, and social statuses associated with reading and writing. Each school develops its own culture (or subculture) of literacy. By the same token, each community containing schools evolves its subculture of literacy.

This use of culture does not imply that there are no cultural traits which subcultures hold in common. Quite the contrary, one way to conceptualize subculture is to see it as a specific adaptive variation that its members make on a small set of underlying cultural themes. This seems to be the case in the subcultures of literacy described to date.

Despite variations among individual schools' cultures of literacy, there are striking similarities. Some of these can be traced to the long tradition of viewing reading and writing as cognitive processes where the important activity is carried out in the heads of individuals (McDermott, 1977; Mehan, 1979). It is hard to find a school that doesn't value formal aspects of reading or writing behavior nearly as much as the decoding or encoding of meaning or that doesn't count the social deportment of readers and writers in evaluating literacy behavior. Furthermore, the vast majority of schools expect the development of literacy skills to occur in a specific sequence of stages; typically simple labeling is succeeded by the ability to deal with "what" questions, and this stage in turn leads to the acquisition of higher order analytic skills.[1]

In the remainder of this paper I describe some of what we have found from our explorations into the culture of literacy. When possible, these findings are supported by or related to recent research conducted from a similar perspective. A final section sketches some of the implications these findings have for educational practices.

Smith

Meanings of Reading and Writing in the Real World

In the real world, reading and writing can be viewed as individual or group adaptive responses, as important roles in the construction of the social order, and as negotiable commodities.

Reading and Writing as Adaptive Responses

Reading and writing, conventional wisdom holds, require certain knowledge and skills that must be taught. This belief, which underlies much educational practice, is reflected in our search for improved pedagogical techniques as well as in the central place methods courses hold in teacher training programs. Ultimately, it represents a kind of "magical thinking" (Emig, in press). Neither the literature describing literacy in other societies (Scribner & Cole, 1978) nor recent research in our own society supports this belief.

For the children she studied, Heath reports

> comprehension was the context rather than the outcome of learning to read. They read to learn something, obtain a desired item or action, and in these situations, they learned to read without formal instruction or the reading-readiness activities generally used by school-oriented parents with preschoolers. (Heath, 1981, p. 9)

This conclusion comes as no surprise to anthropologists. In an environment as literate as ours, where it is virtually impossible to escape regular encounters with printed language, learning to read and write are natural occurrences—"as natural as learning to speak" (Goodman, 1980). Virtually all normal children brought up in the United States, left to their own devices, will do some reading and writing as an adaptive response to the environment.

In this view, people read and write only insofar as these activities fill perceived needs. The reality, predictably, is more complex. Need perception is a highly individual matter, reflecting the idiosyncracies of personal biographies and histories.

Nevertheless, this assumption leads to provocative and fruitful research. Ogbu (1980) argues persuasively that black children frequently do not learn to read and write as readily as their white counterparts because their real life experiences belie the promise of school and of mainstream society that acquiring literacy skills will provide the means to move up and out. They do not remain disadvantaged because they fail to become literate; it is the other way around. The realities of the social caste structure in which they are trapped not only makes acquiring school literacy futile, but also counterproductive to any attempt to breech the imposed ceiling.

On the other hand, Irish working-class families studied in New York City perceived school success to be the only way out of the community (McDermott & Morrison, 1981). As a result, their children were sent to parochial schools at great sacrifice, and every effort was made by parents to see that school expectations were met, even when these expectations ran counter to deeply held values. For example, sometimes teachers would assign homework writing exercises as punishment for misbehavior. Although one mother felt this practice might have the effect of turning her child off to writing, she always insisted the child do it (McDermott & Morrison, 1981).

Watkins encountered families who similarly perceive the acquisition of school literacy and hence the meeting of school expectations as crucial to social advancement. In their attempts to meet these expectations, the families ran into difficulties of a slightly different nature. They were admonished to provide "literate environments" (the particulars of which were spelled out by the school), to read to and with their children, and to check but not correct homework assignments. In the first place, it was never clear where the line between checking and helping should be drawn. More disturbing, however, was the value dissonance this directive created. Their experiences warned them that sending children to school with "incorrect" or "messy" homework frequently resulted in teachers viewing them as illiterate or noncaring parents. Moreover, they ran considerable risk (at least in their own minds) that their children would make negative comparisons between themselves and their teachers if they appeared not to recognize improperly rendered assignments. This was a particularly difficult issue given the strong community value on propriety in act and appearance.

Viewing reading and writing as adaptive responses to perceived needs not only leads to evidence of the differential acquisition of literacy skills and concomitant reactions to school expectation, it also sheds light on a variety of literacy related problems. Few educators view the definition of reading and writing as problematical. Students are classified as readers or nonreaders and writers or nonwriters without much thought about what the classification means. I do not think that such demarcations can be made so easily.

Fiering (1981) took as the starting point for her study one teacher's insistence that her "lower track students did not write"—a major source of frustration in her teaching. Fiering, however, found the classroom to be a beehive of writing activity. Students wrote notes to one another, reminders to themselves, designed word games, drew up contracts, and made lists. When the researcher discussed these observations, the teacher dismissed it with, "Oh, I don't consider that to be writing."

That the teacher chose to count some behaviors as writing, while excluding others that appeared to be similar, came as no surprise. Her definition of writing, which she shares with many educators and parents, precluded her categorizing certain student behaviors as writing. A major goal of enthnographic analysis is to explicate the frameworks or definitions used by members of a culture, and thus to describe how certain people see the world and why.[2]

The fact that teachers count only *some* reading and writing behaviors as actual reading and writing is crucial for understanding the problems involved in describing the culture of school literacy. What counts as reading or writing in school is usually determined by what is taught. Tests are designed for the display not of what may have been learned naturally, but what the teacher believes has been taught. Lessons are planned to systematically lead students through stages that the teacher establishes. Ideally this progression is based on research findings reflecting the experiences of a "representative" sample of learners.

The effects of this counting-only-what-is-taught syndrome on the acquisition and display of reading and writing skills are farreaching. Children coming to school, able as Heath's subjects were to "read to learn," may soon find that what they can do doesn't count as reading. It isn't enough to see words in context and deduce their meanings. Before one can "read" one must learn that, in some mysterious way, print tracks sound. And this is only the beginning. Students will realize that simply encoding meaning in printed symbols, even if the meaning can be retrieved by a reader, doesn't necessarily count as writing. They may have to learn that this print must proceed from left to right, be in a straight line, and meet a number of other formal or functional expectations of the teacher.

Frequently, in order to count as reading or writing, actions must be accompanied by keeping the feet on the floor, assuming an appropriate facial expression, and maintaining total silence. Also, what counts for reading or writing for one student doesn't for another.

Beginning black school readers from Trackton (Heath, 1980) apparently find themselves penalized on reading readiness tests because they cannot answer the "what" question presented by flat, two-dimensional, highly stylized stimuli, even though their past experiences seem to have prepared them to deal with "higher order" analogic questions. The latter skills, presumably, would be overlooked (not counted) because they occur out of expected sequence.

The point is simple. The school culture of literacy typically leads teachers to not count displays of literacy competencies when they do not conform to the definitions and expectations implied in what is taught. Indisputably, these practices are functional, given the sorting role schools play in society. Crucial to educators is the awareness that definitions of literacy vary and are functions of the particular culture (or subculture) of literacy characteristic of schools or communities.

The Role of Reading and Writing in Constructing the Social Order

This essay looks for the answers to school related literacy problems in social organizational rather than in strictly cognitive processes. From a culture of literacy perspective, reading and writing, as cultural phenomena, are important to the construction of social organization.

Culture is not like a suit of clothes to be put on or discarded at will. People don't see the world in a certain way simply because they choose to. They see it the way it has been presented to them, and confirmed by experience. Decisions are made with faith that things are the way they appear through one's cultural lenses.

The culture of literacy, as a way of seeing reading and writing, is no less important. We go to extremes to see that teachers, in their recruitment, training, and assimilation to a school, accept the school culture of literacy. Teachers' "ways of counting" reading and writing behaviors are not simply matters of choice. They reflect how things are from their perspective. Conflicts between cultures, opposing ways of seeing, are resolved at great risk to the individuals committed to them. This goes far in explaining the frustration of both teachers who can't get kids to "learn" and of reformers who can't get teachers to change.

The power of culture is central in understanding the role of literacy in the construction of social organization. Microethnographic efforts at explaining the process of constructing the social organization of classrooms or lessons have made this clear (Mehan, n.d.; McDermott, 1977; Schultz & Florio, 1981; White, 1980). For example, students are commonly grouped or tracked according to reading level. Even in classrooms where the grouping for reading is heterogeneous, teachers' behaviors toward individuals are generally affected by the "known" differences.

Public belief in the importance of developing the kinds of literacy skills presumably offered by schooling is strong. People regularly make decisions about where to live on the basis of the availability of good schools. Literacy is not the only issue prompting these decisions, but it is fundamental. When, for example, a parent explained that she could not enroll her son in the public innercity school because he was "so middle class that he would never survive," her concern was not only for his physical safety but for the quality of preparation he would receive.

Not all parents have options; some simply cannot afford to shop for a school that meets their expectations. Although they may feel just as strongly about the importance of their children developing literacy skills, they are forced to develop a different strategy for assuring it. Some attempt to influence the school. For a variety of reasons such efforts are seldom very satisfying. A more typical response is reactive, and they restructure their lives to conform to school expectations.

The discovery of "community" and its role in schooling may be one of the most significant results of researchers' attention to out-of-school contexts. Obviously, any explanation for the roles literacy plays in real life must take into account the total repertoire of knowledge available "for people to focus themselves on" (McDermott & Morrison, 1981). This means attending to the larger community which both families and schools share in and create.

In literacy research, communities have usually been categorized as school-oriented or nonschool-oriented. School-oriented includes those in which the families' culture of literacy and the schools' are similar and where parents consciously attempt to inculcate in their children appropriate skills, knowledge, and attitudes. Parents frequently make sure their children enroll in schools that will work for them. Our research suggests refining this model, a refinement that will take us a step toward the kind of ethnology of schooling called for by Hymes (1980).

At the risk of oversimplification, I suggest that three configurations of school-community culture types can be identified, based on the way behaviors and attitudes toward literacy are organized. These types can be labeled reactive (where the community organizes its culture of literacy around school expectations), proactive (where the school looks to the community for clues as to how its approach to literacy should be organized), and unrelated (where the families and schools develop their notions in relative isolation one from the other).

The communities investigated to date seem to fit in the following categories:

COMMUNITY CULTURE OF LITERACY TYPES

Reactive   Kingsland (McDermott & Morrison, New York City)
            Shortridge (Watkins, West Philadelphia)
            Roadville (Heath, Southeastern United States)

Proactive	Suburban Public (GSE Graduate Students)
	University Private (University of Pennsylvania Professors)
	School-Oriented (Heath)[3]
Unrelated	Stockton (Ogbu)[4]
	Trackton (Heath, Southeastern United States)

This table throws in relief several interesting facts. First, consistent distinctions do not seem to obtain between white and black communities. Stockton and Trackton are both black and, presumably for the reasons discussed earlier, families from both know that school promises of mobility based on literacy are not to be taken at face value. However, Shortridge is also black, and here the parents, very much like the Irish families in Kingsland, are careful to organize their literacy activities in reaction to school expectations. Apparently, they accept the school promise—or premise.

These divisions do not coincide with either public or private boundaries. Kingsland is parochial, university professors use private schools, and we can assume that Heath's school-oriented families send their children to both private and public schools.

Quite possibly, an understanding of the culture of literacy, reflecting the ways families, individuals, and schools organize their literacy related concerns, can be found only by looking at the community as a whole. Schools and families interact and relate in unique ways to create a culture of literacy. This process must be examined if the meanings of reading and writing in the real world are to be understood clearly.

Reading and Writing as Negotiable Commodities

American educators are obsessed with literacy, particularly reading. Conversations with principals, teachers, and parents about schools almost inevitably turn to the reading level of students. Principals routinely judge the effectiveness of their administrations by changes in the school's annual reading score ranking. Parents evaluate teachers and teachers evaluate parents on how well and how fast students learn to read and write.

Our society's experience is unique only in detail. Historians have warned us that literacy can have different effects and has been put to a wide number of uses by societies in other times and places. Literacy has been used to democratize by breaking up monopolies on knowledge and, by being guarded as the property of a few, also has been used to strengthen or foster elite classes. In our own time we have seen literacy used to disenfranchise voters and to unfairly deny employment. We have also seen political reformers, such as Paulo Freire, promote it as a powerful means for liberation.

To see the full range of uses to which reading and writing can be put requires considering them within the context of a culture of literacy. Such uses vary from community to community and include the availability of the material paraphenalia of literacy, notions of selfworth and one's ability to learn, values attached to the uses of time, and networks of social paths either out of the community or to positions of importance within it. The relationship of schools to the rest of the community is crucial, especially the status of the principals, their knowledge of the community mores, and their notions about literacy.

The remainder of this section will present one case of a school community in Philadelphia. We will see how the principal and community families negotiate a bona fide social contract for the exchange of literacy skills.

The Community

Shortridge, though a black community, hardly qualifies as a typical innercity ghetto. Characterized by extreme social and economic diversity, it has a number of very poor families and a number of socially mobile families in which one or both of the parents hold good jobs. The neighborhood consists mainly of single family dwellings, built a half century ago by Irish and Jewish residents. Some have been converted to house more than one family. During the past fifteen years, the neighborhood has become entirely black, and it is these working-class black families who make up the school community.

The Principal

The principal, an Italian-American native of South Philadelphia, has been at Shortridge for 10 years. Prior to coming he had been vice-principal of a school experiencing a great deal of racial unrest. He distinguished himself, in the eyes of the community and the school district administration, by the skill with which he handled the racial crisis. The respect he gained there followed him to Shortridge.

As a principal he is proud of his school's role in the community. Although he does not reside in the city and neither he nor his staff are much in evidence in the area after school hours, the school is a focal point of community activity. Indeed, it is the central and most visible institution, serving to give a sense of identity to the community. The principal has been very careful to cultivate ties with the parents of his students and with other influential members of the neighborhood.

Not surprisingly, the community relationship to the school is reactive, while the principal's style of interaction with the community would be proactive. He does not hide the fact that he dislikes surprises. His school and office are open to parents and visitors and this contact serves to keep him abreast of problems before they get serious. Through all of his school-community programs he tries to stay a step ahead, to offer before he is asked. In this way he maintains control of the relationship and presents himself as a knowledgeable leader.

He sees the school as an outpost of middle-class culture. His goal is to help as many of the children as possible acquire the trappings of that culture. The success of this mission, he firmly believes, requires that he operate from a position of power. About this he is articulate and certain. Quick and effective solutions to problems demand that they be anticipated and that decisive action be forthcoming. Any move from within the school, from the city administration, or from outside that he sees as a threat to his power is quickly addressed. By most accounts he is a success. He has received several community awards, and the school has been featured in a national publication as a "school that works." He is proudest, however, of the advances his school has made in the city ranking of reading scores, and the number of students who go on to prestigious junior or senior high schools.

Development of literacy skills is seen as central to what he believes is his mission. He proudly proclaims himself an expert in teaching literacy. The school under his direction has participated in a number of innovative language arts programs, and is presently implementing the Pennsylvania Reading Language Arts Program (Botel, 1977).

The Goods

Key to the use of reading and writing skills as "goods" is the academic plus program in the school. This program consists of special classes open to selected good students and is designed to both challenge and reward them. Shortridge, which had been a K-5 school until a sixth academic plus grade was added, offers the option beginning with the fourth grade.

The appeal and the power of academics plus find their roots in the secondary school scene in Philadelphia. Students are offered the choice of two elite schools (one for boys and one for girls), very good academic schools, specialized vocational schools, traditional general schools, and one school-without-walls. Competition is heavy for admission to the "better" schools as well as for some of the private schools in the area.

Selection to academics plus is seen by parents and touted by the school as increasing one's chance of getting into a good school later. The competition starts before children enroll in kindergarten when parents are urged to participate in the school sponsored reading readiness programs. Throughout the early grades it is used as a carrot both to motivate kids to read and to insure that they and their parents develop a proper attitude toward school.

The Negotiation and the Contract

Negotiations start after the teachers have selected students for participation in the program and these choices have been approved by the principal. Officially, selection is open to good students, although the major criterion is attitude.

Appropriate attitude, a complex issue, includes not having been a discipline problem and being cooperative and dependable. In addition, the role parents have played in school life is important in the display of proper attitude. They must be seen as cooperative and caring.

Formal negotiations take place in a meeting between the principal and parents whose children have been chosen to participate. The principal says something like:

> We will do our best to see to it that your children learn to read and write well and will work to get them into good junior and senior high schools if you will work with us.

Working with them means regularly monitoring the children's homework, following a year round program in literacy at home, sending the children to school dressed appropriately, attending parent-teacher conferences, and cooperating with respect to discipline.

The parents are then required to sign a formal agreement containing these provisions. The next year students will be assigned to a special classroom and teacher and will be expected to work at an accelerated pace. Breech of the agreement can result in a student either being put into a regular classroom or not invited to continue for the next grade. Fifth graders who are not selected to the program for the sixth grade must leave Shortridge.

The Results

This case suggests how, through a single program rooted in the community's cultural values on literacy, principals can achieve several goals. They can control the relationship of the school to the community, effectively demand a display of certain attitudes and behaviors, and preclude a number of problems from developing. Through it all, they are consolidating and expanding their own power to influence the behavior of students and parents and to make unpopular decisions of their own. This scenario is possible because the school appears to control a highly valued commodity: Access to facility with reading and writing. Other scenarios, where the participants have different agenda, have been encountered in other school communities. Each has as its basis the amenability of reading and writing (as well as other school-taught skills) to negotiation as a kind of currency.

Implications for Practice

Most teachers and parents have been enculturated into the conventional culture of school literacy. They view reading and writing as essentially cognitive phenomena, and for them the evidence is persuasive. Certain types of students do not do well on reading tests, nor do they give much evidence of wanting to read and write. Even more telling is the evidence provided by those cases where traditional approaches have produced successes; where reading scores have gone up and where children have stopped misbehaving, have learned to love learning, and have graduated to successful adult careers.

At the same time, viewing reading and writing in the real world from the perspective of the culture of literacy reveals a set of processes of which educators and layfolk alike have been unaware. For one thing, major tasks being performed by schools have little to do with learning literacy skills and, for another, children are able to acquire these apart from school efforts (or even despite them). In this light, I propose the following implications for practice emerging from our present understanding of reading and writing in the real world:

1. *A new understanding of children.* Viewing literacy primarily as a cognitive phenomenon leads to a view of children as little more than repositories of competencies. The major concern of schooling becomes the provision, measurement, ranking, and enhancement of these competencies. It can be argued that this is simply fiction. However, the realities of the school culture too often lead to the acceptance of this fiction as reality. It is a short step to believing that what we see children display in classroom interactions, written assignments, oral recitations, and tests is what the children are.

In contrast, the perspective presented here leads us to view children as innately adapting, always seeking to make sense of their world. Thus, they are defined by a delicate and intricate web that extends beyond the classroom in a number of dimensions most of which are not accessible to scrutiny by teachers. Intrusion into this is only done with the utmost sensitivity to the unanticipated risks it might entail.

2. *A sensitivity to children's culture of literacy.* In a paper analyzing "stepping rhymes" used by children, Gilmore (1981) describes one that begins, "Gimmee room." An important

characteristic of this genre of children's play, she notes, is the use of names, which she sees as a tendency to personalize. We would be well served to listen closely to this and other clues children offer to their subculture. Just as the school's culture of literacy is a determinant of how we teach and evaluate reading and writing, so children's subcultures are major influences on what they do or do not do. Of particular importance is the intricate and complex relationship children develop with peers. Only recently have researchers seriously examined children's subcultures where, undoubtedly, the source of many reading and writing problems will be found.

3. *A new appreciation of community.* More school people are seeing themselves as aliens on foreign terrain. From a culture of literacy perspective this is almost never the case. While the relationship between the school and the families it serves may be one of several types, it is always vital. Active engagement in teaching as a process negotiated between community members can lead to its assuming a new significance. Viewing teaching as participation in a community activity can alleviate the isolation many teachers feel and can give them a sharpened sense of their students' real needs. The latter can have the additional effect of removing much of the dependence on outside expertise for answers to questions about discipline, motivation, and technique.

4. *A pedagogy that "gives room."* If reading and writing are in fact adaptive responses, the request of Gilmore's "stepping" girls to "Gimme room!" can be seen as more than a clue to their subcultures. It can be taken as a plea for a new way of teaching. Traditional views of pedagogy view technique as basic. We want to know the best ways to enhance competencies and we want methods to insure that they are displayed to maximum advantage and are fairly evaluated.

Seeing learning as adaptation removes the onus from technique. It puts the emphasis on leaving room for learning. It means making allowances for alternative learning styles—giving opportunity for careful rehearsing before work is displayed in assignments, recitations, or tests. It may mean tolerating some apparent chaos or having sensitivities inadvertently affronted.

In short, this approach calls for extreme sensitivity before intervening in the delicate web defining the child. However, this is not necessarily the same sensitivity a mechanic displays in tuning a motor, a sensitivity born of fear that a false move might upset the functioning of the mechanism. Children are above all human, and sometimes it is necessary to risk upsetting the smooth functioning of the system for the good of the child.

Footnotes

[1] Heath (1981) describes two communities where the preschool child's literacy context leads to either a truncation and limitation of this process or to the development of a different one. Both are shown to lead to problems in school.

[2] In the Fiering study, subsequent investigation revealed the formal properties defining writing that counted as well as enough of the social organization configuration of the classroom to explain some of the reasons why this particular way of counting was functional.

[3] Heath does not claim the status of community for school-oriented families in her paper. She does not contrast school-oriented families discussed in the literature with her Roadville and Trackton communities. Much of this literature reports the experiences of affluent, professional researchers who either studied their own family or families of colleagues.

[4] Ogbu, in the paper cited here, does not claim that he is talking exclusively about Stockton as a community type. He does indicate, however, that many of his contentions are grounded in his Stockton research.

References

Anderson, E. Shortridge school and community: Portrait of the principal. *Ethnographic monitoring of the acquisition of children's reading/language arts skills in and out of school*, D.H. Hymes, principal investigator. Final report to NIE, 1981.

Botel, M. *The Pennsylvania comprehensive reading/language arts plan.* Harrisburg, Pennsylvania: Pennsylvania Department of Education, 1977.

Emig, J. Nonmagical thinking: Presenting writing developmentally in schools. In C. Frederickson, M. Whiteman, and J. Dominic (Eds.), *The nature, development and teaching of written communication, Vol. 2*. Hillsdale, New Jersey: Erlbaum, in press.

Fiering, S. Commodore school: Unofficial writing. *Ethnographic monitoring of children's acquisition of reading/language arts skills in and out of the classroom*. D.H. Hymes, principal investigator. Final report to NIE, 1981.

Gilmore, P. Attitudes and admission to literacy. *Ethnographic monitoring of children's acquisition of reading/language arts skills in and out of the classroom*. D.H. Hymes, principal investigator. Final report to NIE, 1981.

Goodman, Y. *Patterns and processes in young children's reading development.* Paper presented at the Conference Developing Literacy: Young Children's Use of Language, Rutgers University, 1980.

Heath, S.B. The functions and uses of literacy. *Journal of Communication*, 1980(a), *30*.

Heath, S.B. *What no bedtime story means: Narrative skills at home and school.* Paper prepared for the Terman Conference, Stanford University, November 1980(b).

Hymes, D.H. Educational ethnology. *Language in education: Ethnolinguistic essays.* Washington, D.C.: Center for Applied Linguistics, 1980.

McDermott, R. *Problem readers and the social order: Some reasons for focusing on class rooms in reading research.* Paper prepared for National Reading Association Conference, New Orleans, December 1977.

McDermott, R. Achieving school failure. In G. Spindler (Ed.), *Education and cultural processes.* New York: Holt, Rinehart and Winston, 1974.

McDermott, R., & Morrison, A. *Literacy and learning in a community framework.* Final report to NIE of New York City study of Literacy for Learning. H. Lichter, principal investigator, 1981.

Mehan, H. The competent student. Typed manuscript, n.d.

Mehan, H. *The structure of classroom events and their consequences for students' performances. In P. Gilmore (Ed.), Ethnography and education: Children in and out of school.* Washington, D.C.: Center for Applied Linguistics, 1981.

Ogbu, J.U. *Literacy in subordinate cultures: The case of black Americans.* Paper presented at the Conference on Literacy, Library of Congress, Washington, D.C., July 1980.

Scribner, S., & Cole, M. Literacy without schooling: Writing for intellectual effects. *Harvard Educational Review,* 1978, *48.*

Schultz, J.J., Florio, S., & Erickson, F. Where's the floor? Aspects of the cultural organization of social relationships in communication at home and at school. In P. Gilmore (Ed.), *Ethnography and education: Children in and out of school.* Washington, D.C.: Center for Applied Linguistics, 1981.

Watkins, M. Shortridge school and community: Teacher-parent relationships. *Ethnographic monitoring of children's reading/language arts skills in and out of school.* D.H. Hymes, principal investigator. Final report to NIE, 1981.

White, J. *The construction of knowledge in a social studies class.* Unpublished doctoral dissertation, University of Pennsylvania, 1980.